VOCABULARY BASICS FOR BUSINESS

Barbara G. Cox, Ph.D.

ID0206810

JOB SKILLS

NETEFFECT SERIES

Prentice Hall

Upper Saddle River, New Jersey 07458

Library of Congress Cataloging-in-Publication Data
Cox, Barbara G., 1946-
    Vocabulary basics for business / Barbara G. Cox.
       p. cm.—(NetEffect series. Job skills)
    ISBN 0-13-060710-X
       1. Business—Terminology.   I. Title.   II. Series.
    HF1002.5 .C69 2003
    650'.01'4—dc21

                                    2002074939

Publisher: Stephen Helba
Executive Editor: Elizabeth Sugg
Editorial Assistant: Anita Rhodes
Managing Editor: Mary Carnis
Production Management: Ann Mohan, WordCrafters Editorial Services, Inc.
Production Liaison: Brian Hyland
Director of Manufacturing and Production: Bruce Johnson
Manufacturing Manager: Cathleen Petersen
Creative Director: Cheryl Asherman
Senior Design Coordinator: Miguel Ortiz
Marketing Manager: Tim Peyton
Composition: Pine Tree Composition, Inc.
Printer/Binder: Phoenix Book Tech
Copyeditor: Amy Schneider
Proofreader: Patricia Wilson
Cover Design: Christopher Weigand
Cover Printer: Phoenix Book Tech

Pearson Education Ltd.
Pearson Education Australia Pty. Limited
Pearson Education Singapore Pte.Ltd.
Pearson Education North Asia Ltd.
Pearson Education Canada Ltd.
Pearson Educación de Mexico, S.A. de C.V.
Pearson Education—Japan
Pearson Education Malaysia, Pte. Ltd.
Pearson Education, Upper Saddle River, New Jersey

Copyright © 2003 by Pearson Education, Inc., Upper Saddle River, New Jersey 07458. Portions of the new product were previously published as VOCABULARY BASICS by Paradigm Publishing, Inc. © 1993. All rights reserved. This publication is protected by Copyright and permission should be obtained from the publisher prior to any prohibited reproduction, storage in a retrieval system, or transmission in any form or by any means, electronic, mechanical, photocopying, recording, or likewise. For information regarding permission(s), write to: Rights and Permissions Department.

Prentice
Hall

10 9 8 7 6 5 4 3 2 1
ISBN 0-13-060710-X

Contents

19 Suffixes: Naming   137

20 Section 3 Review   144

Preface

Vocabulary Basics for Business is intended for adults who wish to improve their English vocabulary. The most common reason for needing to increase or broaden vocabulary is lack of experience with reading. Not surprisingly, thoughtful reading is key to developing a broader vocabulary. Read as much as you possibly can read—anything that interests you, whether magazine or novel, textbook or junk mail, a newspaper or a cereal box, e-mail or Web pages—read.

When you read, watch for unfamiliar words or phrases or words used in unfamiliar ways. Try to determine their meaning by the other information you are given in the sentence or paragraph. Re-read a paragraph and state it in your own words. Start by thinking, "This paragraph says that . . ." or "This probably means. . . ."

Re-read. If you find reading a textbook somewhat difficult, read a few pages and then go back and read them again. Many times your knowledge of the topic will increase as you read further, so that when you re-read earlier material you understand it more easily and clearly.

Using a dictionary to check the meaning of a word is worth the time. Keep a dictionary handy. Look up meanings of words that you come across in your reading and then use that meaning to re-state the information in a way that is clearer to you. Looking up words just for fun is not necessarily a useful exercise because you do not see or hear the terms used in a sentence or paragraph—that is, "in context." Your understanding and your memory are much better when you see a term in a specific context.

One of the important ways that this book will help you increase your vocabulary is to teach you ways to think about what you read and about words and their relationships. In that way, *Vocabulary Basics for Business* is a tool that supports and facilitates—that is, makes easier—the vocabulary development work you do through your reading.

Vocabulary Basics for Business approaches vocabulary development in two ways:

through strategies, or plans, for building vocabulary, and

through reading, understanding, and using specific words.

Your primary goal in "Section 1: Clues from Context" is to learn to determine word meanings from surrounding information. You will use your common sense to ask questions about what you read that will help you decide what it means. You will notice and interpret "signals" that may help you understand a new term. The signals include definitions, comparisons and examples, opposites and contrasts, and cause and effect. The approaches are not difficult, but they are often overlooked.

The strategy you will learn in "Section 2: Word Families" is to examine how words are related, how they compare with one another and how they differ, how their meanings are similar and what they have in common. You will contrast words and groups of words in a lesson that uses words related to communication. In a lesson that presents words related to sizes and amounts, you will examine relationships among words that share a common idea; that is, you will put words "in order." In a third lesson in this section, you will examine shades of meaning among words that share a concept or idea. In this case, you will compare and use words about importance. Taken together, the three lessons in Section 2 will help you learn to compare and contrast words, categorize them, and put them in order as strategies for thinking about new words and becoming more familiar with them. These lessons depart from some of the traditional approaches to vocabulary building, so have fun with them.

The strategy you will learn in Section 3 is word analysis. You will become familiar with a basic set of prefixes, roots, and suffixes—word parts. Knowledge of the meanings of word parts and how they combine to form various words will give you a distinct advantage when you encounter new words or new uses of words.

In "Section 4: Troublemakers," you will practice using words that are often confused or misused, from *accept* through *prerequisite*. These terms, like others throughout the text, are presented in various contexts to reinforce and clarify their use by example.

You will learn and use specific business terms in the final eleven lessons of *Vocabulary Basics for Business*. This section includes topics that are common to most businesses, including human resources, sales and marketing, accounting and finance, shipping, business computing, and leadership. You will encounter target business terms in sample business documents such as ads, announcements, memos, letters, and spreadsheets. The goal for Section 5 is not for you to develop a thorough mastery of a huge number of business terms. Rather, you will master a reasonable number of terms common to the business areas and be introduced to others. You will also learn how some everyday terms have particular meanings in business contexts.

Each section of *Vocabulary Basics for Business* opens with a short introduction and a self-assessment that will give you a preview of the lessons in that section. The answers to the self-assessment are presented immediately after the questions.

The lessons have many questions and exercises to help you understand and practice the strategies and terms. Answers and explanations for all of these are included in the book, with the exception of the five review chapters.

Too often students have been asked to acquire or extend their language without connecting it to their lives, interests, and other learning. Building vocabulary should be an adventure beyond the classroom, not an exercise limited by it.

ACKNOWLEDGMENTS

Several reviewers made valuable suggestions for improving this text, which are gratefully acknowledged. These reviewers are:

Mary Walton
Carteret Community College

John O'Brien
Adams State College

Joseph D. Chapman
Ball State University

Thanks also to Elizabeth Sugg for her ready laugh and to Jerry Cox and Alice Gilland, who were quick with encouragement and never complained about dinner being late.

Barbara G. Cox, Ph.D.

Section 1
Clues from Context

One of the most important ways we determine the meaning of words is from their context, the information contained in the surrounding words and sentences. You already use context to understand familiar words. Consider the use of the word *file* in the following sentences:

- His assistant put the agreement in his personal *file*.

- She used a *file* on the rough edges.

In which sentence does *file* mean "folder" or "drawer"? In which sentence does it mean "a tool for smoothing"? The only way to distinguish between the two uses of these words is to pay attention to their context—that is, the information surrounding them in the sentences.

In Section 1 of *Vocabulary Basics*, you will learn some ways to use context to help you figure out an unfamiliar word's meaning. The context often provides direct, helpful hints. Some types of hints we use to determine meanings include

- commonsense questions,

- definitions,

- comparisons and examples,

- opposites and contrasts, and

- cause and effect and other logical relationships

WHAT DO YOU KNOW?

TRUE OR FALSE?

Circle T or F to indicate whether each of the following statements is true or false. On a separate sheet of paper, state why you chose that answer.

T F   1. The context of an unfamiliar word or phrase can help you figure out its meaning.

T F   2. The only way to learn the meaning of an unfamiliar word is to look it up in a dictionary.

T F   3. In some sentences, comparisons and examples can give hints about the meaning of an unfamiliar word or phrase.

T F   4. Opposites or contrasts for an unfamiliar word are not every helpful.

MULTIPLE CHOICE

Circle the letter next to the best answer for each question. On a separate sheet of paper, state why you chose that answer.

1. Which of the following choices signals that a definition or explanation is coming?
   - (a) if/then
   - (b) not
   - (c) in short
   - (d) similar to

2. Which of the following choices signals that an opposite or contrast is coming?
   - (a) if/then
   - (b) not
   - (c) in short
   - (d) similar to

3. Which of the following choices signals that a comparison is coming?
   - (a) if/then
   - (b) not
   - (c) in short
   - (d) similar to

4. Which of the following choices signals that a cause-and-effect clue is coming?
   - (a) if /then
   - (b) not
   - (c) in short
   - (d) similar to

HOW DID YOU DO?

True or False: (1) T; (2) F; (3) T; (4) F
Multiple Choice: (1) c; (2) b; (3) d; (4) a

Commonsense Questions

Often you can understand the general meaning of a word by applying your common sense and background knowledge. Using your experience and existing knowledge to guess about an unfamiliar word—or a familiar word used in an unfamiliar way—is often enough for you to understand the idea, instruction, or information you are reading. You will be able to satisfy your purpose for reading. This approach allows you to keep on reading, and your understanding of the term may well improve as you continue to read.

To apply this "commonsense" strategy, follow three steps:

1. Be aware of words that are unfamiliar to you. This may sound somewhat simplistic, but often you can read and understand unfamiliar words from their context without really stopping to think about them. To make words part of your active, working vocabulary, you need to be aware of them.

2. Ask yourself commonsense questions suggested by the context. Think about other information in the sentence and paragraph that gives you a general idea about the meaning of the unfamiliar word.

3. Try to answer your questions in simple terms, using words you know well. Then restate the sentence using your own words. In this way you will transfer the general meaning of the term into your thinking. (Also, when you later check on the specific definition of the

term in a dictionary or glossary, this information will help you decide which definition is most appropriate. It will help you remember the word's meaning the next time you see it.)

The following examples provide some commonsense questions and answers. These examples show how commonsense questioning will help you understand unfamiliar words and phrases.

- The bus driving safety regulations *prohibit* drivers from talking with passengers while operating the vehicle.

  Possible question: What would safety regulations have to say about drivers talking to passengers while driving?

  Answer: They probably would forbid talking so the driver would pay attention to driving. *Prohibit* means "forbid."

- The company purchased new equipment to replace the *obsolete* machinery they had used for twenty years.

  Possible question: Why would a company replace old machinery?

  Answer: The old machinery might still work, but it could be outdated. New equipment might work faster or have more features. *Obsolete* means "outdated."

WHAT DO YOU KNOW?

Now try the next two examples yourself. Write a definition of the italicized word in each of the following sentences, using the blank space provided.

1. The international club had members of *diverse* backgrounds.
   Possible question: What kinds of backgrounds would members of an international club have?
   Diverse: _____

2. The college's *criteria* for admissions included high academic achievement and high scores on the entrance exams.
   Possible question: How do colleges decide which students to admit?
   Criteria: _____

HOW DID YOU DO?

1. Their backgrounds would be varied or different. *Diverse* means "varied."

2. Colleges set requirements or standards to use to evaluate applicants. *Criteria* are *standards.*

This approach will not work well when the sentence or passage does not have enough clues to help you ask useful questions or make sensible guesses about the meaning. In those cases you may need to refer to a dictionary before reading further.

Working with Words

TRUE OR FALSE?

Circle T or F to indicate whether the statements that follow each numbered sentence are true or false. Use the sentence context and your common sense to decide.

1. The workers were glad to hear that their new pay increases were retroactive to the beginning of the previous month. (*Hint:* Why would the timing of a pay increase make workers happy?)

   T   F   The pay increase would not begin for two months.

   T   F   The workers would receive additional pay for work they had already been paid for.

2. The experts were hired to enhance the computer system so that it could prepare additional types of reports. (*Hint:* Could the computer already do everything needed?)

   T   F   The computer system was removed and a new one installed.

   T   F   The original computer system did not do everything the company wanted it to do.

3. The office used the constructive suggestions immediately. (*Hint:* What type of suggestions would be used immediately?)

   T   F   The suggestions were silly.

   T   F   The suggestions were probably practical.

   T   F   The suggestions were just complaints and not very useful.

Now use your own commonsense questioning for the remainder of the items.

4. The rules prohibited using the office telephones for personal calls.

   T   F   Employees were not allowed to use the telephones for personal calls.

   T   F   The rules forbid using the telephones for personal calls.

5. The manufacturer wanted to expedite shipping the goods because the customers needed them in a hurry.

   T   F   The manufacturer wanted to rush the goods to the customer.

   T   F   The manufacturer wanted to stop shipping.

6. Please verify that all items on the bill were actually purchased.

   T   F   You are being asked to pay the bill.

   T   F   You are being asked to make sure you are not being charged for something that was not purchased.

7. The diverse shapes, sizes, and colors gave the candle buyers many choices.

    T F   There are many different styles of candles.

    T F   The candles are large.

8. The firm wanted to expand its customer service department so it could serve more customers.

    T F   The customer service department was serving enough customers.

    T F   The firm wanted to make the customer service department larger.

9. The supervisor's decision was not impartial; he gave special consideration to his nephew.

    T F   The supervisor had no favorites; his decision was fair.

    T F   The supervisor's decision was influenced by his relationship with his nephew.

10. Due to her inquisitive nature, Ms. McComas was often asking "why?"

    T F   Ms. McComas wanted more knowledge.

    T F   Ms. McComas liked to make inquiries—that is, to ask questions.

FILL IN THE BLANKS

From the following list, select the word that best completes each sentence and write the word in the blank provided. Use the sentence context to help you decide. Use each word only once. Use all of the words.

constructive	diverse	enhance
obsolete	prohibit	verify

1. John Garcia could do many jobs because of his _____ skills.
2. The criticisms were not very _____; they were not practical or realistic.
3. The nonsmoking office workers wanted management to _____ smoking.
4. The committee decided to replace the longtime president, saying that his ideas were _____.
5. The accounting clerk's job was to _____ the amounts on the sales slips.
6. The graphs were added to _____ the appearance of the report.

USING YOUR WORDS

Use each of the following words in a sentence that demonstrates that you understand the meaning of the word.

1. prohibit

2. constructive

3. enhance

4. obsolete

5. verify

6. diverse

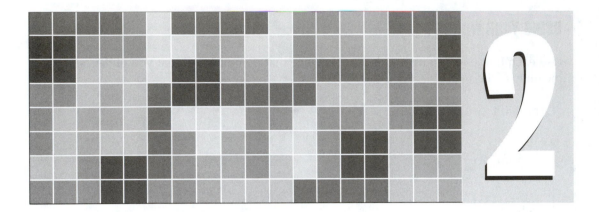

Definitions

Definitions of unfamiliar words are sometimes provided for you. This kind of information context is usually very direct and easy to find. This lesson will help you learn to recognize when a definition is given for an unfamiliar or new word.

APPOSITIVES ("NEXT-TO" WORDS)

In some cases, a definition is placed after an unfamiliar term and is separated from the rest of the sentence by commas, dashes, or parentheses. Alternatively, the definition is placed before the new term, and the new word is separated from the rest of the sentence. The part that is set off by commas is said to be an *appositive* or to be *in apposition*. *Apposition* comes from word segments meaning *next to*; the word or phrase is *next to* its definition or label.

- The vitamins were advertised as having highly *salubrious*—healthy— effects for most adults.

   Even if you are not familiar with the word *salubrious*, you learn its meaning from the definition, which is separated from the rest of the sentence by the dashes. *Salubrious* means "healthy."

- The property will *depreciate*, decrease in value, when the noisy new highway is built nearby.

    The meaning of *depreciate* is given by the phrase set off by the commas. *Depreciate* means "to decrease in value."

WHAT DO YOU KNOW?

Now try the next two examples yourself. Write a definition of the italicized word in each of the following sentences, using the blank space provided.

1. Due to their *negligence*, their extreme carelessness, the plastic melted and the project was ruined.
      negligence: _____
2. The shipment of goods, the *consignment*, arrived four days late.
      consignment: _____

HOW DID YOU DO?

1. *Negligence* is defined for you by the word *carelessness*.
2. A *consignment* is a *shipment* of goods.

SIGNAL WORDS

Sometimes "signal words" indicate that a definition is coming. The simplest of these is the word *or*. Other signals are *and, that is, in short,* and *in other words*.

- The office manager agreed to buy pens that were comparable, or similar, to the ones they used previously.

    Comparable is defined in the sentence by the word *similar*. The signal word is *or*.

WHAT DO YOU KNOW?

Now try the next two examples yourself. Write a definition of the italicized word in each of the following sentences, using the blank space provided. Circle the signal word or phrase in each case.

1. Her job performance was *deemed*, or considered, to be the best in the company.

    deemed: _____

2. The *frequency* of her *tardiness*—in other words, how often she was late—created problems on the job.

    frequency: _____

    tardiness: _____

HOW DID YOU DO?

1. *Deemed* is explained by the word *considered*. *Deemed* means "considered." The signal is the word *or*.
2. The definition of *frequency* is "how often"; the meaning of *tardiness* is "lateness." The signal is the phrase *in other words*.

EXPLANATIONS

Sometimes longer explanations, rather than definitions, provide the context you need to understand a word or phrase. Explanations are not always preceded by a signal word or phrase, so be alert.

- The manager was *ignorant* of the facts. The staff had not provided her with the necessary information.

    The explanation that the staff had not given her information tells us that *ignorant* means "uninformed" or "unaware."

WHAT DO YOU KNOW?

Now try the next two examples yourself. Write a definition of the italicized word in each of the following sentences, using the blank space provided.

1. The machine operator was *negligent*. He did not pay attention to what he was doing.

    negligent: _____

2. The comments were *irrelevant*. They had nothing to do with the topic under discussion.

    irrelevant: _____

HOW DID YOU DO?

1. The explanation that the operator did not pay attention tells us that *negligent* means "inattentive" or "careless."

2. In this example, *irrelevant* means "*unrelated*" or "*not pertinent.*"

Working with Words

MULTIPLE CHOICE

Circle the letter next to the answer that best completes the sentence. Use the definition in the sentence to help you determine the best answer. Underline the signal that tells you to watch for a definition.

1. Just as they had been for years, the customary steps were followed—that is, the _____ procedures were carried out.
   - (a) harmful
   - (b) usual
   - (c) customer's
   - (d) new

2. The animals looked healthy. They exhibited, or _____, no symptoms of disease.
   - (a) exchanged
   - (b) hid
   - (c) earned
   - (d) showed

3. The director of financial accounting ordered that the firm's extra funds be disbursed to, or _____, deserving employees.
   - (a) distributed to
   - (b) hidden from
   - (c) taken from
   - (d) shown to

4. By their mutual, or _____, agreement, the two firms combined to form one.
   - (a) short
   - (b) false
   - (c) insurance
   - (d) joint

5. The driver did not maintain the van properly. An accident occurred when the brakes failed and the driver was fined for negligence, or _____.
   - (a) poor vision
   - (b) unnecessary speed
   - (c) careless neglect
   - (d) drugs

6. The smokers were warned that smoking is detrimental, injurious, and dangerous to their health—in short, _____.
   - (a) effective
   - (b) hated
   - (c) harmful
   - (d) crafty

7. The bank would not cash the check due to insufficient funds in the account, in other words, _____.
   - (a) there was no signature on the check.
   - (b) the account was too old.
   - (c) there was not enough money in the account.
   - (d) it was the wrong bank.

8. The consignment, or _____, was delivered to the wrong address.
   - (a) shipment of goods
   - (b) connection
   - (c) signature
   - (d) employee

USING YOUR WORDS

Use each of the following words in a sentence that also gives its meaning. Refer to the lesson and the preceding exercise as needed.

1. customary

2. exhibited

3. negligent

4. insufficient

5. comparable

6. frequency

Comparisons and Examples

Two types of context clues are presented in this lesson: *comparisons* and *examples*. You will learn to identify the signals that indicate comparisons and examples and to use these two types of clues to determine the meaning of unfamiliar terms.

COMPARISONS

Clues to meanings of unfamiliar words or phrases are sometimes found in the context of a comparison. When the information given in the comparison is familiar to you, your common sense will guide your understanding. (However, when the information is also unfamiliar, you will need to use other resources such as a dictionary, an instructor or friend, or continued reading.) A comparison will usually, though not always, be introduced by a signal word or phrase.

Signals that alert you to a comparison include *as*, *as _____ as*, *like*, *just as*, and *similar to*. Can you think of any others? Examine the following example.

- "Never!" the speaker *rasped*, sounding similar to the filing of finger-nails.

  Fingernail filing creates a scraping or harsh rubbing sound. In this example, *rasp* means "make a rough, harsh sound." (By the way, the noun *rasp* is a tool for filing or grating. The verb *rasp* means to make that sound.)

WHAT DO YOU KNOW?

Try the next two yourself. Circle the letter next to the answer that best defines the italicized word. Use common sense and the context clues of comparison to help you decide. Underline the signal that tells you to watch for a comparison.

1. He made his wishes as *explicit* as large handwriting on a wall.
   - (a) unrealistic
   - (b) obvious
   - (c) quietly
   - (d) sweet
2. Like a banker weighing gold, she measured the shelves with great *precision*.
   - (a) exactness
   - (c) rulers

HOW DID YOU DO?

1. Large handwriting is very obvious; *explicit* means "obvious." The signal is *as* _____ *as*.
2. A banker weighs gold very carefully, exactly. *Precision* means "exactness." The signal is *like* _____.

You may occasionally find a comparison introduced by the phrase *not unlike* or *no different than/from*.

WHAT DO YOU KNOW?

In the following examples, circle the letter next to the answer that best defines the italicized word. Use common sense and the context clues of comparison to help you decide. Underline the signal that tells you to watch for a comparison.

1. The *confrontation* between the two managers during the panel presentation seemed no different than a fight between spoiled ten-year-olds.
   (a) breakfast   (c) argument
   (b) discussion   (d) table

2. Not unlike bargaining at an outdoor market, the *negotiating* required some give and take on both sides.
   (a) charity   (c) changes
   (b) bargaining   (d) relay

HOW DID YOU DO?

1. This sentence compares a confrontation to a fight; the best answer is *argument*. The signal words are *no different than*.

2. This sentence compares negotiating to bargaining; the best answer is *bargaining*. The signal words are *not unlike*.

EXAMPLES

Many times you can determine the meaning of a term from examples. If you use your common sense, experience, and background knowledge to figure out what the examples have in common, you should have a good idea about the meaning of the main word or phrase.

Signals That an Example Is Coming

The signal words and phrases *for example, for instance, examples include, such as,* and *including* are usually accompanied by one or more examples. Sometimes the word *like* is also used as a signal of example.

- Be sure to label all containers with *inflammable* contents, such as gasoline, alcohol, kerosene, or natural gas.

Gasoline, alcohol, kerosene, and natural gas all catch fire easily. They are examples of things that are inflammable. In this example, *inflammable* contents means contents that can catch fire easily.

WHAT DO YOU KNOW?

Try the next two examples yourself. Circle the letter next to the answer that best defines the italicized word. Use common sense and the context clues of example to help you decide.

1. That group of architects is known for designing many *edifices,* including houses, office high rises, hotels, and apartment complexes.
   - (a) cabins
   - (b) hospitals
   - (c) buildings
   - (d) roads

2. The committee made many *amendments* to the agreement. For example, they increased the minimum pay, decreased the minimum hours, restricted the telephone service, and expanded the sales territories.
   - (a) changes
   - (b) provisions
   - (c) additions
   - (d) amenities

HOW DID YOU DO?

1. All of the examples are buildings. *Edifices* are *buildings.*
2. All of the examples are changes; *amendments* are *changes.*

More Signals

Other example clues are signaled by the terms *especially, particularly, in particular,* and *specifically.* Also, watch for phrases like *among the most* (*least, best,* etc.) or signals of number.

WHAT DO YOU KNOW?

Circle the letter next to the answer that best defines the italicized word.

1. The company appreciated all the employees' *endeavors* to meet the deadline, especially the hours they worked nights and weekends.
   (a) efforts   (c) thresholds
   (b) positions   (d) entreaties

2. Among the most important *benefits* to the new employee were good health insurance coverage and sick leave.
   (a) advantages or "extras" provided by an employer
   (b) day care for workers' children
   (c) compositions
   (d) nurses in the building

HOW DID YOU DO?

1. This sentence gives *working nights and weekends* as an example of an endeavor; an *endeavor* is an *effort.*
2. The *benefits* listed are examples of *advantages or "extras" provided by an employer.*

A List as an Example

Sometimes, instead of a signal word, a list of examples is itself the signal.

WHAT DO YOU KNOW?

Circle the letter next to the answer that best defines the italicized word. Use common sense and the context clues of example to help you decide.

1. The most common forms of *remuneration* for work in that company are weekly salary and cash bonuses.
   (a) vacation   (c) pay
   (b) recognition   (d) schedule

2. The firm bought new machinery, new delivery vans, and a piece of property for a larger building. These *acquisitions* were costly and used all the firm's savings.
   (a) positions   (c) bills to pay
   (b) trucks   (d) newly obtained items

HOW DID YOU DO?

1. The examples of *remuneration* are salary and bonuses. *Remuneration* is *pay.*

2. Machinery, vans, and property that are all new are listed as examples of acquisitions. *Acquisitions* are *newly obtained items.*

More on Examples

Like the other contextual clues you have learned, examples can help you decide between two or more meanings of a word that may already be familiar.

WHAT DO YOU KNOW?

The following examples use the word *deductions* with different meanings. Example clues will help you understand which way the word is being used. Circle the letter next to the answer that best defines the way *deductions* is used in each sentence. Use common sense and the context clues of example to help you decide.

1. The *deductions* from her paycheck included a health insurance premium, a charitable contribution, and income tax withholding.
   (a) additions of money
   (b) decisions
   (c) hours worked
   (d) amounts of money taken out

2. Watsmith looked over the evidence. "From these clues, I have concluded that the thief was a man. I have figured out that the thief worked alone and that he wore gloves."
   "Wonderful *deductions,* Watsmith!" exclaimed his friend.
   (a) amounts taken out
   (b) suit of clothes
   (c) conclusions
   (d) mystery

HOW DID YOU DO?

1. The examples of *deductions* are all *amounts of money taken out* of the check.
2. The examples of *deductions* are the *conclusions* that Watsmith reached based on the clues.

Working with Words

MULTIPLE CHOICE

Circle the letter next to the answer that best defines the italicized word. Use common sense and the context clues of comparison and example to help you decide. Underline the signal that tells you to watch for a comparison or example.

1. Like a jeweler cutting a diamond, the machine cut the patterns with great *precision.*
   (a) messiness
   (b) exactness
   (c) frequency
   (d) loudness

2. Like an argument between parents distresses children, the angry *confrontation* between the managers made others in the room uncomfortable.
   (a) argument
   (b) door
   (c) wedge
   (d) hug

3. Just as research helps scientists make educated guesses, the information about the problem led them to make several intelligent *deductions* about its cause.
   (a) chemicals
   (b) more money
   (c) conclusions
   (d) none of the above

4. The small *remuneration* for the work was almost like getting no money at all.
   (a) bribe
   (b) pay
   (c) work
   (d) penalty

5. The *benefits* were changed to include dental insurance, more vacation days, and life insurance.
   (a) rules of a factory
   (b) calendars of meetings
   (c) expenses related to work
   (d) "extras" from an employer

6. They tried many ways to get the information. Their *endeavors* included volunteer hours on the phone and surveys at shopping centers.
   (a) efforts
   (b) lunches
   (c) premiums
   (d) pay

7. The company made several *acquisitions* last year, including new equipment and new office furniture.
   (a) purchases
   (b) mistakes
   (c) targets
   (d) moves

8. We need to make *amendments* to the claim; for instance, we need to change the amount claimed and rewrite the description of the damage.
   (a) deliveries
   (b) transmissions
   (c) changes
   (d) signatures

FIND THE MISFIT

In each group, underline the word that does not belong with the others. Then state why it doesn't belong. The first one is done for you as an example.

1. argument, confrontation, <u>contraction</u>, fight

   A contraction is not a type of fight.

2. purchase, manage, acquisition, property

3. endeavors, attempts, efforts, clues

4. precision, exactness, presence, care

5. obvious, explicit, free, clear

USING YOUR WORDS

Use each of the following words in a sentence. Include an example or comparison to help make the meaning clear.

1. explicit

2. amendments

3. endeavors

4. deductions

5. remuneration

6. confrontation

Opposites
and Contrasts

Statements that include contrasts or opposites often provide valuable information to help you understand new words. Contrasts and opposites tell us how things are different. By using a clue about what a word or phrase is not, you can judge what the word or phrase might be. In this lesson, you will learn to judge the meaning of unfamiliar words or phrases by using clues of opposites and contrasts.

NOT

A common signal for an opposite is the word *not*.

- The value of the stock was definitely not going up. It wasn't even staying the same. In fact, it was *plummeting*.

  If the stock value was not going up and it wasn't staying the same, then plummeting must mean going down or falling. *Plummeting* means "falling very quickly."

WHAT DO YOU KNOW?

Now try the next two examples yourself. Write a definition of the italicized word in each of the following sentences, using the blank space provided. Underline the signal that tells you to watch for an opposite.

1. Attendance at the meeting was *optional*, not required.

    optional: _____

2. Harold's work was not sloppy, it was *meticulous*.

    meticulous: _____

HOW DID YOU DO?

1. Since attendance was not required, it was the individual's own decision or choice. *Optional* means "not required" or "voluntary."

2. Harold's work was not sloppy; therefore, it must have been neat or precise. *Meticulous* means "very precise about details."

DESPITE, ALTHOUGH, UNLIKE, AND IN CONTRAST TO

Other words and phrases that signal an opposite or contrast in meaning include *despite*, *although*, *unlike*, and *in contrast to*.

WHAT DO YOU KNOW?

Using these clues, write a definition of the italicized word in each of the following sentences, using the blank space provided.

1. Despite his great *anxiety* about the job interview, Mr. Carson appeared to be relaxed and calm.

    anxiety: _____

2. Though Alice was a *competent* carpenter, she was very poor with numbers.

    competent: _____

HOW DID YOU DO?

1. Mr. Carson looked calm, even though he was not. Emotional states that contrast with calm might include anger, nervousness, or excitement. Since it is not likely that Mr. Carson would be angry about a job interview, we might conclude that he was nervous. Indeed, to have anxiety is to be worried, nervous, or fearful.
2. Alice is not very good with numbers. This lack of ability is not true of her carpentry, however, in which she is capable, or competent.

NONETHELESS, BUT, AND HOWEVER

Nonetheless, *but*, and *however* are other words that signal a contrast.

WHAT DO YOU KNOW?

Using these clues, write a definition of the italicized word in each of the following sentences, using the blank space provided.

1. The work in those two offices is *equivalent*, but the pay is different.
    equivalent: _____
2. The office was in close *proximity* to Celia's house; however, it was a long drive in the heavy traffic.
    proximity: _____

HOW DID YOU DO?

1. We know that the pay for work in the two offices is not the same; the pay is different. The signal word *but* tells us that the work itself is in contrast to the pay; therefore, we can conclude that the work is the same. In short, the work is the same, or equal, but the pay is different.
2. Does Celia live near her office? If so, the drive to work should be a short one. The sentence tells us that the drive is a long one, and the signal word *however* tells us this is contrary to what we expect. The drive is a long one, but the office is near. Your common sense and the contrast signal tell you that *proximity* means "nearness."

CONTRASTS IN TIME

Since changes occur from past to present and from present to future, sometimes contrasts are established between what was, what is, and what will be. One signal for these differences is the word *formerly*; another is *previously*. *Now* and *in the future* also signal possible contrasts, as do *in the past* with a phrase such as *but now*, and *before* and *after*.

WHAT DO YOU KNOW?

Write a definition of the italicized word in each of the following sentences, using the blank space provided. Underline the signals that tell you to watch for contrast in time.

1. The office was in close *proximity* to Ann's house before she moved; now she lives an hour's drive away.

    proximity: _____

2. A signature on this form was previously *optional*; now it is required.

    optional: _____

HOW DID YOU DO?

1. How do you know that *proximity* means "near"? What signal was used for contrast?

2. How do you know that *optional* means "not required"? What signal was used for contrast?

Working with Words

MULTIPLE CHOICE

Circle the letter next to the answer that best defines the italicized word or phrase. Use the context clues of contrast to help you decide. Underline the signals that tell you to watch for a contrast.

1. While the production materials were inexpensive, the finished goods were very *dear*.
   - (a) good
   - (b) distant
   - (c) costly
   - (d) useful

2. Contributions to the charity were *optional*. Most employees made a donation even though it was not required.
   - (a) high
   - (b) elective
   - (c) observed
   - (d) due

3. The house was *in close proximity* to the park but far from shopping centers.
   - (a) above
   - (b) comparable
   - (c) near
   - (d) measured

4. Rather than being related to the issues, the politician's remarks were *irrelevant*.
   - (a) unrelated
   - (b) meddlesome
   - (c) rude
   - (d) humorous

5. The two brothers were very different. While one was *meticulous* about everything, the other paid no attention to details.
   - (a) precise
   - (b) calculating
   - (c) angry
   - (d) direct

6. While everyone else in the meeting was relaxed, the presenter was feeling some *anxiety*.
   - (a) intelligence
   - (b) nervousness
   - (c) sincerity
   - (d) chill

7. The number of items was *equivalent*; however, the quality was not the same.
   - (a) equal
   - (b) valuable
   - (c) large
   - (d) double

8. The action they took was hasty and unwise; it was not *prudent*.
   - (a) slow
   - (b) important
   - (c) wise
   - (d) free

9. The employer looked for *competent* workers, not ones without ability.
   - (a) energetic
   - (b) able
   - (c) intelligent
   - (d) self-motivated

10. After months of refusing to agree to management's terms, the workers finally *capitulated.*
    (a) gave in   (c) left work
    (b) filed suit   (d) went home

FILL IN THE BLANKS

From the following list, select the word that best completes each sentence and write the word in the blank space provided. Use the contrast in the sentence to help you decide. Use each word only once. Use all of the words.

irrelevant	competent	proximity	anxiety	dear
meticulous	optional	equivalent	capitulate	prudent

1. The team did not have to practice on Saturday or Sunday; weekend practice was _____.

2. The committee was very _____ in its review of the financial reports; it did not miss a single number.

3. The department store goods were formerly very _____, but now their prices are very reasonable.

4. Although he was nervous before the test, after it began he had no _____.

5. The sales manager thought that changing advertising agencies was a good idea, but the executive committee decided that it would not be _____.

6. Art gave his supervisor many reasons to change the decision, but the supervisor would not _____.

7. I cannot go far to work; the factory must be in close _____ to my residence.

8. While they put in the same number of hours, their pay was not _____.

9. Janet performed the job very poorly; she was not _____.

10. She continued to give answers that had nothing to do with the questions. Her responses were _____.

USING YOUR WORDS

Use each of the following words or phrases in a sentence. Include a contrast to help make the meaning clear.

1. competent

2. prudent

3. optional

4. close proximity

5. anxiety

Cause and Effect

Statements expressing cause-and-effect relationships provide useful context information to help you interpret unfamiliar words or phrases. Cause-and-effect relationships tell us *what happened* (the effect or result) and *why it happened* (the cause). For example, in the sentence, "The plastic melted because the temperature was too high," the result is that the plastic melted; the cause is the high temperature. In this lesson, you will learn to reason about word meanings by using cause-and-effect clues together with your common sense and experience.

IF/THEN

Cause and effect is often associated with *if/then* or *when/then* statements. The *then* is sometimes omitted, but it is still understood.

WHAT DO YOU KNOW?

Use context clues to interpret the italicized word in each of the following sentences. Write a definition in the blank space provided.

1. If you practice keyboarding every day, (then) you will become more *proficient* at data entry.

    proficient: _____

---

2. If you do not write more clearly, (then) your ideas will need further *clarification*.

    clarification: _____

3. When you *remit* payment, (then) the collection agency will stop sending you the overdue notices.

    remit: _____

HOW DID YOU DO?

1. Practicing a skill or activity usually helps someone improve that skill. To become more proficient, then, means to become more skilled or better able.

2. When ideas are not expressed in a way that is understandable, they need more explanation. Clarification is making something more clear or understandable.

3. A collection agency sends letters and overdue notices when a bill has not been paid. The agency stops sending the notices when the payment is sent. To remit means to send and usually refers to sending payment.

THUS, THEREFORE, CONSEQUENTLY, SO, AND RESULTING

Thus, therefore, consequently, so, and *resulting* also signal an effect or result of an action or thought.

WHAT DO YOU KNOW?

Write a definition of the italicized word in each of the following sentences, using the blank space provided.

1. The large post *obscured* part of their view of the stage, so Jim missed seeing some of the action.

    obscured: _____

2. Victoria felt that the information was *insufficient* and, therefore, postponed the decision until more data was available.

    insufficient: _____

HOW DID YOU DO?

1. Jim could not see all of the stage because the post was in the way; it hid part of the stage. In this example, *obscure* means "to cover" or "to hide."
2. Victoria waited to get more information; she did not have enough to make her decision. *Insufficient* means "not sufficient" or "not enough."

BECAUSE, SINCE, AS, OR DUE TO

Look for signal words *because*, *since*, *as*, or *due to* as indications of cause. They signal that information is being provided that will tell you why something happens or is true.

WHAT DO YOU KNOW?

Use logical thinking to interpret the italicized word in each of the following sentences. Write a definition in the blank space provided.

1. She was fined because the equipment was not being operated in *compliance* with safety regulations.

    compliance: _____

2. Since the *compensation* for his new job is higher, Ray now earns enough money to make payments on a new car.

    compensation: _____

HOW DID YOU DO?

1. A fine is usually paid as a result of a violation. To be in compliance, then, means to be in conformity or agreement with—in this case, in accordance with the regulations.
2. A job with higher compensation is one that pays more; compensation is payment.

SO THAT, IN ORDER THAT, AND IN ORDER TO

Some sentences express purpose or intention, and their interpretation is related to cause-and-effect reasoning. Common signals of purpose are the phrases *so that* and *in order that* (or *in order to*). In these cases, the "cause" follows the signal.

WHAT DO YOU KNOW?

Use context clues to interpret the italicized word in each of the following sentences. Write a definition in the blank space provided.

1. Fran took on an extra job in order to *augment* her meager salary.
   augment: _____
2. The driver took an *alternate* street so that he could avoid the roadblock.
   alternate: _____

HOW DID YOU DO?

1. If Fran needed an extra job because her salary was very small, she needed to increase her income. *Augment* means to "increase" or "make greater."
2. If the driver needed to avoid a blocked road, he would choose a different road. In this case, *alternate* means "substitute" or "second choice."

Working with Words

MULTIPLE CHOICE

Circle the letter next to the answer that best defines the italicized word or phrase. Use common sense and the context clues of cause and effect to help you decide. Underline the signal that tells you to watch for a cause or effect.

1. The engineers needed to modify the equipment so that it would be *in compliance with* government regulations.
   (a) in violation of
   (b) in accordance with
   (c) in payment of
   (d) in compromise with

2. The bank closed Anna's checking account due to *insufficient* funds.
   (a) counterfeit
   (b) lack of
   (c) unavailable
   (d) lateness

3. Barry added a loudspeaker to the system in order to *augment* the sound level.
   (a) add to
   (b) change
   (c) decrease
   (d) modulate

4. The attorneys added several items of *clarification* to the contract so that the clients would better understand the terms of the agreement.
   (a) cost
   (b) adjudication
   (c) explanation
   (d) restriction

5. Since she was *proficient* with the accounting spreadsheet computer program, her supervisor assigned her the most difficult spreadsheet tasks.
   (a) skilled
   (b) happy
   (c) new
   (d) frustrated

6. Cristina did not *remit* her payments by the deadline, and consequently her insurance was canceled.
   (a) collect
   (b) reprimand
   (c) send
   (d) request

7. Donald's speech *obscured* the facts, resulting in a poorly informed audience.
   (a) told
   (b) hid
   (c) spent
   (d) obtained

8. The doctor donated her services to the free clinic; thus, no *compensation* was due her.
   (a) appreciation
   (b) compromise
   (c) time sheet
   (d) payment

9. If the present method does not solve the problem, (then) you will need to try an *alternate* approach.
   (a) different
   (b) chance
   (c) altruistic
   (d) methods

10. They labeled each product with a colored tag so that they could *differentiate* them from one another.
    (a) reproduce   (c) distinguish
    (b) package   (d) subtract

FIND THE MISFIT

In each group, underline the word that does not belong with the others. Then state why it doesn't belong.

1. augment, intensify, increase, fight

2. send, pay, rebut, remit

3. unseen, hidden, obscured, related

4. efficient, expensive, proficient, skilled

5. deteriorate, differentiate, distinguish, discriminate

USING YOUR WORDS

Use each of the following words in a sentence. Include the cause-and-effect signal indicated in parentheses to help make the meaning clear.

1. augment (since)

2. insufficient (because)

3. proficient (so that)

4. clarification (in order to)

5. remit (if/then)

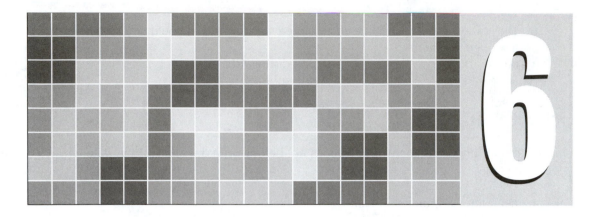

Section 1 Review

The lessons in Section 1 presented several ways to examine the context that surrounds unfamiliar words or phrases in order to determine their meaning. The types of hints presented in these lessons included the following:

- commonsense questions
- definitions
- comparisons and examples
- opposites and contrasts
- cause-and-effect and other logical relationships

In this lesson, you will review approaches to using contextual information.

COMMONSENSE QUESTIONS

Use your experience and existing knowledge to help you determine the meaning of unfamiliar words or phrases.

1. Be aware of words that are unfamiliar to you. Underline them, circle them, or make a list of them.

2. Ask questions about the context. Think about the information given in the sentence or paragraph.

3. Try to answer your questions in simple terms using words you know well. Restate the sentence in your own words.

DEFINITIONS

Often a sentence or paragraph provides the definition of an unfamiliar word for you. Look for definitions set off by commas, in parentheses, or dashes. Also, look for words that signal that a definition is coming, such as the following:

or	and	that is
in short	in other words	

COMPARISONS AND EXAMPLES

Comparisons can provide valuable information about meanings of words and phrases. Use your common sense when you evaluate a comparison. Look for words that signal that a comparison is coming, such as the following:

as	as _____ as	like	just as
not unlike	no different than/from	similar to	

Many times you can determine the meaning of a term from examples provided in the text. Use your common sense, experience, and background knowledge to evaluate what the examples have in common. Sometimes examples are simply listed. Other times, however, signal words are used, such as the following:

for example	for instance	examples include
such as	including	like
especially	particularly	in particular
specifically	among the most (least, best, etc.)	

OPPOSITES AND CONTRASTS

Statements that include contrasts or opposites often provide valuable information. Use a clue about what a word or phrase is *not* in order to judge what the word or phrase might be. Common signals of opposites and contrasts include the following:

not	despite	although
unlike	in contrast to	nonetheless
but	however	

Sometimes contrasts are established according to what was, what is, and what will be. These contrasts are almost always indicated by a signal word, such as the following:

formerly	previously	before
now	presently	in the future
in the past	but now	after
but then		

CAUSE AND EFFECT

Cause and effect is often associated with *if/then* or *when/then* statements. (The word *then* is often omitted.) Other signals of a cause-and-effect relationship include the following:

thus	therefore	consequently
resulting	because	since
as	due to	therefore
so that	in order to	hence

Working with Words

QUESTIONING

Each of the following sentences contains an italicized word. A series of questions follows each sentence. Decide which questions will help you use your common sense to determine the meaning of the italicized word. For each question, circle U if the question is useful; circle N if the question is not useful.

1. The store tried to *expedite* shipping the appliances because the buyers were in a hurry.

    U N   What does a store try to do for customers who are in a hurry?

    U N   Why were the buyers in a hurry?

2. The shopping center decided to *expand* its parking lot to have room for the increasing number of customers.

    U N   What was the goal of the shopping center in doing this to its parking lot?

    U N   What can be done to parking lots to make more room?

    U N   Why were there more customers?

3. Since the report looked boring, Gina added charts and graphs to *enhance* its appearance.

    U N   What was in the charts and graphs?

    U N   What would adding charts and graphs do to the appearance of a boring report?

4. The suggestions were very *constructive*; they were practical, easy to follow, and would lead to a better product.

    U N   Are practical suggestions that lead to a better product considered helpful?

    U N   What kinds of things can suggestions be?

5. The *obsolete* equipment was replaced with modern machinery.

    U N   What kind of equipment would be replaced with modern machinery?

    U N   Is it expensive to buy new equipment?

TRUE OR FALSE?

Circle T or F to indicate whether each of the following statements is true or false. On a separate sheet of paper, state why you chose that answer.

1. The manager admonished the employee for his poor work habits.

    T F   The manager did not care about the employee's work habits.

    T F   The manager scolded the employee.

2. She accrued so many debts that year that she could not pay them all.

   T   F   She paid all her bills each month.

   T   F   Her debts added up over time.

3. George required close supervision, but Ray worked well autonomously.

   T   F   Ray did car repairs.

   T   F   Ray worked independently.

4. Susan was known for her brevity; her reports were always short.

   T   F   Susan talked too much.

   T   F   Susan was brave.

5. Their conclusion, which was based on conjecture, turned out to be wrong.

   T   F   They knew magic.

   T   F   They had all the facts.

MULTIPLE CHOICE (DEFINITIONS)

Circle the letter next to the answer that best defines the italicized word. Use context clues to help you decide which answer is best. Underline the signal that tells you to watch for a definition.

1. The report was completed in haste and was *replete* with, or _____, errors.
   - (a) sent with
   - (b) copied with
   - (c) full of
   - (d) revised with

2. They frequently asked the elderly woman because she was known for her *sagacity*, or _____, for advice.
   - (a) beauty
   - (b) wisdom
   - (c) stew
   - (d) birthplace

3. The rest and relaxation had a *salubrious*, or _____, effect on the over-worked manager.
   - (a) healing
   - (b) dangerous
   - (c) political
   - (d) patriotic

4. The judge threatened to *revoke* his license if he drove over the speed limit again. In other words, his license would be _____.
   - (a) canceled
   - (b) temporary
   - (c) expensive
   - (d) expired

5. The many pages of his writing were evidence that Sean took *copious* notes at the meeting. In other words, he took _____ notes.
   - (a) many
   - (b) someone else's
   - (c) sacred
   - (d) sloppy

MULTIPLE CHOICE (COMPARISONS AND EXAMPLES)

Circle the letter next to the answer that best defines the italicized word. Use the context clues of comparison and example to help you decide. Underline the signal that tells you to watch for a comparison or example.

1. The new employee was as *gregarious* as a politician at a fund-raising party.
   (a) gristly   (c) sociable
   (b) agrarian   (d) tall

2. Like peas in a pod, their answers were nearly *identical*.
   (a) alike   (c) green
   (b) toothy   (d) correct

3. The changes in the organization were *premature*, like unripe fruit.
   (a) forgotten   (c) too soon
   (b) too late   (d) too serious

4. An example of her *procrastination* was that she repeatedly put off doing the reports.
   (a) writing   (c) sour attitude
   (b) delaying   (d) height

5. Gossip can be as *malicious* as the curse of an evil witch.
   (a) masculine   (c) true
   (b) juicy   (d) spiteful

MULTIPLE CHOICE (OPPOSITES AND CONTRASTS)

Circle the letter next to the answer that best defines the italicized word. Use the context clues of opposite and contrast to help you decide. Underline the signal that tells you to watch for an opposite or contrast.

1. Because her intentions were *explicit*, not hidden, they could predict her answer.
   (a) unknown   (c) good
   (b) bad   (d) obvious

2. His response was *ambiguous*; it was not clear.
   (a) indefinite   (c) large
   (b) no   (d) black

3. The advice was very *prudent*; it was not reckless.
   (a) ready   (c) jolly
   (b) expensive   (d) cautious

4. Unlike her co-workers who were often late, Sally was always *punctual*.
   - (a) doubtful
   - (b) on time
   - (c) empty-headed
   - (d) prepared

5. His brother was *parsimonious*, but Jorge was quite generous.
   - (a) vegetarian
   - (b) ceremonious
   - (c) stingy
   - (d) married

MULTIPLE CHOICE (CAUSE AND EFFECT)

Circle the letter next to the answer that best defines the italicized word. Use the context clues of cause and effect to help you decide. Underline the signal that tells you to watch for a cause or effect.

1. Because Ben was *preoccupied* with other matters, he did not listen carefully.
   - (a) thinking about
   - (b) tired of
   - (c) out of town for
   - (d) deaf

2. The accounting statement was the *preliminary* one; therefore, another statement would be distributed showing the final numbers.
   - (a) preparatory
   - (b) wrong
   - (c) lined
   - (d) written

3. The company performed preventive maintenance on all the delivery vans in order to *preclude* possible problems in the future.
   - (a) ignore
   - (b) keep
   - (c) avoid
   - (d) mainstream

4. Her excuse was *plausible*, so her supervisor believed it.
   - (a) probable
   - (b) detailed
   - (c) long
   - (d) on time

5. If the funds had been *allocated* properly, then everyone would have received a fair share.
   - (a) stolen
   - (b) filed
   - (c) distributed
   - (d) spent

USING YOUR WORDS (REVIEW)

Use each of the following words in a sentence that also gives its meaning.

1. disbursed

2. determined

3. negligence

4. frequency

Use each of the following words in a sentence. Include a comparison, example, or contrast signal to help make the meaning clear.

1. explicit

2. precision

3. endeavors

4. amendments

5. optional

6. equivalent

Use each of the following words in a sentence. Include a cause-and-effect signal to help make the meaning clear.

1. remit

2. insufficient

3. clarification

4. proficient

Section 2
Word Families

Section 2 of *Vocabulary Basics* groups words into *families*, words that are related because they express related ideas. While you continue to build familiarity with a set of words for future understanding and use, you will examine relationships among words, using techniques that can be applied to many concepts and word families as you continue to develop your verbal abilities.

Three ways to think about words are covered in these lessons:

- contrasts
- categories
- shades of meaning

In Lesson 7, you will contrast words and groups of words about communicating. Words about sending and receiving, positive and negative communications, and asking and answering are among those covered. The importance of communications in today's society cannot be overemphasized. Technological developments have made the communication of messages faster and wider-reaching than ever before.

In Lesson 8, you will examine relationships among words that describe size and amount, categorize them, and put them "in order." You will learn that some words meaning "big," "small," "many," or "few" are usually used in specific situations. We call a small sum of money *paltry*, but we wouldn't call a small animal or person or house *paltry*.

In Lesson 9, you will compare words that describe importance, which are not easily put in order and are often used only in certain contexts. Importance is not a concrete entity that can be weighed and measured. Consequently, words related to this concept must express the "weight" of importance through differences in meaning that may be subtle or slight, but significant. You will examine words related to degrees of importance and understand differences in shades of meaning.

WHAT DO YOU KNOW?

TRUE OR FALSE?

Circle T or F to indicate whether each of the following statements is true or false. On a separate sheet of paper, state why you chose that answer.

T F 1. All words are neutral. They become positive or negative only by virtue of the way they are used.

T F 2. *Imply* refers to what a speaker does. *Infer* refers to what a listener does.

T F 3. *Excessive, exorbitant, extravagant,* and *immoderate* all mean "too many" or "too much."

T F 4. The words *some, several,* and *numerous* are in order of quantity, from fewest to most.

MULTIPLE CHOICE

Circle the letter next to the answer that best completes the sentence.

1. Because the speaker _____ from his topic, the audience had difficulty following his logic.
   (a) delineated   (c) revealed
   (b) digressed   (d) dictated

2. The _____ child was smaller than his playmates, but was healthy and happy.
   (a) miniature   (c) diminutive
   (b) heavy   (d) puny

3. The _____ feature of the product is its ease of use.
   (a) urgent   (c) salient
   (b) eminent   (d) imminent

HOW DID YOU DO?

True or False: (1) F; (2) T; (3) T; (4) F
Multiple Choice: (1) b; (2) c; (3) c

Communication

The English language has a huge number of words that are related to communicating. This may be because verbal communication, language, is uniquely human and important to our lives. Today's world, especially, is very aware of the importance of communicating clearly. The "information age" emphasizes giving and receiving information more quickly, to and from more people, and in more ways.

This lesson teaches you to think about words related to communication by grouping them into categories and by considering how they are similar or different.

TWO-WAY OR ONE-WAY COMMUNICATION

One common meaning for the word *communicate* is "interchange thoughts or information"—usually by writing or speaking on one side and reading or listening on the other. This view of communication means a process that is two-way.

Communicate is also used to mean only one part of the process: the telling, informing, or asking side of the activity.

The following words are related to *communicate*. Which ones can be classified as two-way? Which are one-way?

exchange	inform	explain	converse	declare	listen
correspond	write	interact	ask	instruct	read

Exchange, converse, correspond, and *interact* require two people (or more), and we could describe them as being two-way actions. The words *inform, explain, declare, write, act,* and *instruct* refer only to the speaker or writer, and we might categorize these as one-way actions. The remaining two words, *listen* and *read,* are also one-way activities.

SENDING OR RECEIVING

Many more words represent one-way actions than two-way actions. The "one-way" words may themselves be categorized in different ways. One pair of categories is "sending," or words that are related to writing or telling, and "receiving," or words that are related to reading or listening. How would you categorize the italicized words in the following sentences?

- After reading the report three times, he began to *comprehend* its meaning.

  > *Comprehend* means "understand." We would put it in the "receiving" category.

- The bank *apprised* the couple of the penalties for late payment.

  > *Apprise* means "inform" or "notify." We would put it in the "sending" category.

- Although George did not state directly that Gail was older than she admitted, he *implied* that she was.

  > *Imply* belongs in the sending category; the speaker or writer does the implying. *Imply* means "hint"; it signifies that there is more than what is being said directly.

- We *inferred* from Larry's comments that Gail was older than she said.

  > *Infer* belongs in the receiving category; the reader or listener does the inferring. *Infer* means "draw a conclusion by logic or reasoning, without being told directly."

POSITIVE OR NEGATIVE COMMUNICATION

Some words that indicate communication convey a positive or negative intention. *Scold, criticize,* and *mock,* for example, deliver a negative message to the listener. On the other hand, *praise, compliment,* and *cheer* deliver a positive message. How would you categorize the italicized words in the following sentences? Remember to use your common sense to help you determine each word's meaning.

- The supervisor *admonished* the clerk for his poor performance.

Since the clerk's performance was poor, the supervisor's communication would probably deliver a negative message. Indeed, *admonished* means "scolded" or "reprimanded."

- Ruth's chief *commended* her for her quick action during the crisis.

    Ruth's chief would probably not scold her for quick action in a crisis, but praise her. *Commend* means "praise" or "compliment" and has a positive message for the hearer.

ASKING OR ANSWERING

Some communication words can be categorized as *asking* or *requesting*; others refer to *answering* or *responding*. Make a list of words that can be categorized as asking words. Here's a start:

beg, inquire, _____

How would you categorize the italicized words in the following sentences?

- The officer began to *interrogate* the witnesses.

    Commonsense questioning tells us that the police officer would be questioning the witnesses. *Interrogate* means "question."

- Elizabeth *refuted* the accusations, giving evidence that they were untrue.

    Showing that the accusations were untrue was Elizabeth's way of responding to them. *Refute* means "demonstrates the falsity of a statement."

FOCUSED OR WANDERING COMMUNICATION

Certain words indicate wandering from the subject; they mean that the speaker does not make sense or is not precise. To *babble*, for example, indicates speaking nonsense; to *murmur* indicates speaking in a way that is not easily understood. To *focus* or *emphasize* is not wandering but being direct and to the point. How would you categorize the italicized words in the following sentences?

- The speaker was careful to *delineate* the plan very clearly.

    Delineate means "outline," which helps to focus information or make it clear.

- During her presentation, she began to *digress* and talk about other topics.

  Digress means "wander from the topic or point of a communication."

OTHER CATEGORIES

Many other categories could be made for words related to communication. Use your creativity and imagination to devise some. What words in the communication word family can you think of that are informal or formal? That usually refer to writing rather than speaking, and vice versa?

How might you categorize the following words?

whisper   shout   mumble   scream   yell   murmur   blast

One category for all the words in this list is *voice loudness*.

COUSINS

We have been looking at *verbs*, but many *adverbs* and *adjectives* are frequently used to describe communications.

How are the following adjectives related? What do they have in common? (Use a dictionary to check meanings if you are not sure.)

1. brief   concise   wordy   long-winded   redundant
   condensed   terse   compact   voluminous

2. polite   nasty   diplomatic   politic   cautious
   kind   critical   angry   mean

The first list contains words indicating the length of communications, whether they are long or short. The second list has words related to polite or impolite tone.

Communications come in many forms and by way of various means. Make a list of all the written and spoken forms you can think of. Which has more? Here's a start:

Written Communications
letter   book   poem

Spoken Communications
chat   speech   scolding

Now make a list of the *means* of communicating. Are there more for written or for spoken communications? Here's your start:

Means of Communicating
telephone   delivery   service   mail

Working with Words

MULTIPLE CHOICE

Circle the letter next to the answer that best completes the sentence.

1. June's instructor _____ her for submitting her paper on time.
   (a) commended   (c) apprised
   (b) comprehended   (d) professed

2. Because the speaker _____ from his topic, the audience had difficulty following his logic.
   (a) delineated   (c) revealed
   (b) digressed   (d) dictated

3. The classroom teacher _____ the students about who cheated on the test.
   (a) refuted   (c) inferred
   (b) directed   (d) interrogated

4. The manager _____ that she would not recommend anyone for a promotion.
   (a) implied   (c) inferred
   (b) interrogated   (d) dictated

5. Although the speaker did not tell them the actual cost, the audience
   _____ that it was very high.
   (a) implied   (c) inferred
   (b) interrogated   (d) dictated

6. When the supervisor _____ the staff of the possible layoffs, they became
   angry.
   (a) admonished   (c) apprised
   (b) digressed   (d) directed

7. We asked the executives to _____ the steps of their plans for the future of
   the company.
   (a) delineate   (c) imply
   (b) interrogate   (d) digress

8. The foreman _____ his workers for not cleaning the machinery properly.
   (a) digressed   (c) apprised
   (b) admonished   (d) refuted

FIND THE MISFIT

In each group, underline the word that doesn't belong with the others. Then state why it doesn't belong. Each group represents one of the following: sending, receiving, asking, answering, positive, negative, direct, indirect.

1. interrogate, inquire, request, infer

2. admonish, scold, admit, criticize

3. digress, wander, babble, instruct

4. comprehend, hear, read, state

5. read, reply, refute, respond

6. infer, understand, inform, listen

7. delineate, praise, state, tell

8. comprehend, commend, praise, laud

9. imply, hint, indicate, request

10. apprise, assert, claim, comprehend

FILL IN THE BLANKS

From the following list, select the word that best completes each sentence and write the word in the blank space provided. Use the sentence context to help you decide. Use each word only once. Use all of the words.

commend	delineate	imply
apprise	digress	admonish

1. I would like to _____ you of the fact that there will be no increases in pay this year.
2. I do not mean to _____ that you do not deserve them.
3. Indeed, I _____ you on your good work.
4. When you make your speech, do not _____ from the main topic.
5. Please _____ the steps of the new procedure for us.
6. My supervisor will _____ me for being late.

USING YOUR WORDS

Use each of the following words in a sentence that demonstrates that you understand the meaning of the word.

1. imply

2. infer

3. delineate

4. digress

5. refute

Size and Amount

The English language provides a wealth of word choices that enable us to express ourselves in very precise ways. Variations in meaning from one word to another that seem slight or insignificant may have special importance when we need to communicate accurately and effectively.

In this lesson, you will learn to distinguish among words related to size and amount and to use them appropriately. Some of these words differ from one another in *degree*; that is, one word is slightly more or less of something than another. For example, *tiny* indicates something slightly smaller than *small*. Some words related to size and amount differ from one another because they are most often used in particular contexts. *Wee*, for example, is often used to describe elves or leprechauns ("the *wee* people"), or in Scottish dialogue referring to infants ("*wee bairn*"). *Paltry* is often heard in reference to money, as in "a *paltry* sum"—an amount of money that is not worth much.

IN ORDER OF SIZE

How big is big? How small is tiny? Some words about size can be put in order, from small to large or the reverse. Look at the following word groups. Number the words in each group from 1 to 3, with 3 being the word that indicates the largest size.

a. _____ big   b. _____ large

    _____ huge   _____ giant

    _____ immense   _____ gigantic

For most people, the meanings of the words in the two lists probably grow in size as they proceed from top to bottom.

Other size words are more difficult to put in order. How would you order the following? Do your classmates agree?

a. _____ enormous   b. _____ mammoth

   _____ tremendous   _____ colossal

   _____ monumental   _____ stupendous

The words in these two groups do *not* clearly differ by degree. There is no absolute order.

Now consider these words related to *small*. Number the words in each group from 1 to 3, with 3 being the word that indicates the largest size.

a. _____ minute   b. _____ microscopic

   _____ tiny   _____ miniature

   _____ small   _____ little

Again, the words probably increase in size from top to bottom. But what about the following words?

teeny   wee   tiny

While many people would agree that *tiny* is probably the largest of these three words, *teeny* and *wee* are difficult to put in order of size. Some of our size words differ from one another in usage or context; that is, they vary in meaning rather than degree or order. While the differences may not seem significant, they are important for accurate, precise communicating. *Short, long,* and *tall,* for example, refer to height or length, not weight, volume, or area. We say "tall building" but not "tall farm"; we say "short person" but not "short price." *Thin* and *fat* often refer to girth (how big around), but *thin* also refers to thickness. A few more examples are presented in the following sections. Can you think of others?

Large

Ample has fairly broad applications, referring to extent, amount, or size. *Ample* can mean plentiful or sufficient. We say "ample size" (an elephant), "ample financial reserves" (a healthy bank account), or "ample food" (plenty to eat). We do not use it to refer to height or length. (An *ample* person is large but not necessarily tall; a snake is not usually *ample,* though it may be very long.)

Massive denotes something that is large and heavy, whereas *huge* denotes something that is large in bulk but may or may not be heavy. A mountain boulder may be both huge and massive; a giant kite may be huge, but it is not usually considered to be massive.

Spacious means "big and roomy" and refers to large spaces such as rooms, buildings, and outdoor areas: *spacious* office, *spacious* hotel, *spacious* ranch.

Small

Diminutive frequently refers to people (and sometimes animals), indicating relatively small physical size or a slight build. It indicates someone who is small and thin but within normal range. *Puny* also refers to people and animals, and sometimes plants, but indicates something or someone small and feeble or underdeveloped. A diminutive child is small but not necessarily unhealthy; a puny child may be underfed and weak as well as small.

Minute (pronounced "my-NOOT") looks very much like *miniature*. *Minute* is used to indicate something very fine or small, as in "*minute* particles of dust." *Miniature*, on the other hand, indicates a small version of something that is ordinarily larger. *Miniature* furniture is used in dollhouses; model airplanes are *miniature* versions of the real vehicles.

Trivial and *petty* mean "insignificant." *Trivial* can imply commonplace, and often refers to issues, questions, or matters: The committee ignored the *trivial* matter. *Petty* commonly indicates lack of importance: "*Petty* cash" refers to a minor amount of money kept for small expenses; "*petty* larceny" refers to a theft of something considered less valuable than "grand larceny."

IN ORDER OF AMOUNT, NUMBER

Some terms we use to describe an amount, supply, or number are *relative*—that is, more or less than the next term. They can be put in order. The words in each of the following lists are in order; they proceed from the smaller to the larger amount or number.

- some, several, numerous
- multiple, many, countless
- adequate, abundant
- none, rare, few

Words describing frequency, or how often something happens, can also be put in order. How would you order the following words from least frequent to most frequent?

often   never   sometimes   rarely

Most people would agree on this order: never, rarely, sometimes, often.

Many, Much, Enough

Terms we use to indicate *many* include *some*, *several*, *various*, *multiple*, and *numerous*. *Countless* means so many that they cannot be counted, as do *myriad* and *innumerable*.

Abundant and *copious* are most commonly used to refer to a very large supply of something: The country's *abundant* oil resources made it rich. The student took *copious* notes of the lectures. *Abundant* and *copious* mean more than enough, more than adequate, or more than sufficient. (*Enough*, *adequate*, and *sufficient* are used almost interchangeably; they do not vary by degree.)

Too Many, Too Much

Excessive, *exorbitant*, *extravagant*, and *immoderate* all mean "too many" or "too much."

Excessive is used in the broadest range of contexts and meanings and means "more than what is needed or required": The police officers were accused of using *excessive* force when they arrested the suspect.

Exorbitant is usually used to mean "more than is fair," as in "*exorbitant* prices."

Extravagant is most commonly encountered in relation to spending or purchases: The new coat was an *extravagant* purchase.

Immoderate is often used in the context of lack of judgment or reason where moderation should rule, as in "*immoderate* eating" or "*immoderate* drinking."

Few, Little

Paltry indicates an amount having little value, worth, or importance: "A *paltry* sum" or "a *paltry* amount of money" is not much money. *Measly* also means "having little value": The firm gave its managers a *measly* 2 percent pay increase.

Meager indicates lacking in quantity or quality: The *meager* meal did not satisfy her hunger.

Two nouns that mean lacking in number or amount are *paucity* and *dearth*. *Paucity* is used in more situations than *dearth*; *paucity* can refer to lacking in number (a *paucity* of trees or a *paucity* of students) or to lacking in amount (a *paucity* of oil). *Dearth* often refers to a scarcity or lack of food.

Working with Words

FILL IN THE BLANKS

From the following list, select the word that *best fits* the meaning of each sentence and write the word in the blank space provided. Use each word only once. Use all of the words. (*Hint:* First, complete the items you are sure of; then complete the more difficult ones.)

petty	diminutive	miniature	spacious
puny	enormous	minute	massive

1. They tried to move the executive's _____ desk, but it was too heavy.
2. The architect's model of the proposed shopping center included _____ buildings and trees.
3. The _____ child was smaller than his playmates, but was healthy and happy.
4. Pay for the stamps with _____ cash.
5. Most of the offices were small; the executives' offices, however, were very _____.
6. The report was very thorough; it provided _____ details about the company's daily operations.
7. The tree was not just big, it was _____.
8. The plants had not received proper care and looked very _____.

MORE WORDS

Make a list of the words you can think of that mean "small" or "little" and another list of words that mean "large." You will probably be surprised at how many you can name. Compare your list with those of your classmates. Make a group list.

FILL IN THE BLANKS

From the following list, select the word that *best fits* the meaning of each sentence and write the word in the blank space provided. Use each word only once. Use all of the words. (*Hint:* First, complete the items you are sure of; then complete the more difficult ones.)

meager	adequate	abundant	petty
extravagant	paltry	exorbitant	paucity

1. You can buy all of this for the _____ sum of $4.

2. The staff wondered why the managers were making such a fuss over a matter that seemed so _____.

3. The company's _____ financial resources were used to invest in new products.

4. Buying the expensive new suit was _____, but he did it anyway.

5. Is there _____ space for everyone to be comfortable?

6. The prices at that stationery store are _____; we no longer buy our supplies there.

7. Mrs. Hubbard's supply of dog bones was very _____.

8. There seemed to be a _____ of applicants qualified for the job.

FIND THE MISFIT

In each group, underline the word that does not belong with the others. Then state why it doesn't belong.

1. extravagant, expensive, exasperate, exorbitant

2. trivial, pursuit, paltry, meager

3. adequate, spacious, enough, sufficient

4. minute, massive, heavy, large

5. puny, small, underfed, old

6. diminutive, slight, dim-witted, small

Importance

In this lesson, you will put words in order of "how much" of something they represent. The concept of *importance* and words that tell us *how* important will be explored in more detail. Many words that are not related to size or amount can be put in some logical order of degree. In fact, when we make comparisons with *more* and *most*, or *less* and *least*, we are indicating degree. For example, consider the meanings of *frequent, more frequent, most frequent*, or *frequent, less frequent, least frequent*. The order of frequency is quite clear; we know which phrase indicates *most* often and which indicates *least* often.

Another way degree is indicated is with the word endings *-er* and *-est*. Consider *fast, faster, fastest* or *bright, brighter, brightest*. Which is more *fast* or more *bright*? (When we use these forms to indicate differences, we are using *comparative* forms. Sometimes we refer to the *more* and *-er* forms as *comparative* and to the *most* and *-est* forms as *superlative*.)

Other groups of related words can be put in order of degree without using comparative forms of the words. In the following lists, which word is "more" than the others?

satisfactory, good, wonderful

annoyed, angry, furious

In the first list, the degree of goodness increases from left to right. In the second list, the degree of anger increases from left to right.

WHAT DO YOU KNOW?

Look at the following word groups. Number the words in each group from 1 to 3, with 3 being the word that indicates the *most* of what is described.

a. words that mean *damaged*
_____ scratched
_____ demolished
_____ dented

b. words that mean *talk*
_____ speak
_____ shout
_____ whisper

c. words that mean *frighten*
_____ terrify
_____ surprise
_____ scare

HOW DID YOU DO?

Determining "which is more" in these cases is not difficult. Thinking about words in this way can help you develop an appreciation of words and their distinctions. Most people would order them like this:

   (a) 1, 3, 2; (b) 2, 3, 1; (c) 3, 1, 2

IN ORDER OF IMPORTANCE

Which is more important: *serious* or *urgent*? Most of us would agree that *urgent* is more important. Like so many concepts or ideas, importance is relative. Some things are more important than others. Our language has many words that express varying degrees and types of importance.

WHAT DO YOU KNOW?

Are the following words *not important, very important,* or *important?* Fill in the blanks, using each word only once. (*Hint:* Fill in the *not important* words first, then the *very important* words; finally, fill in the remaining "middle" words.)

essential	insignificant	worthless	urgent	serious
significant	notable	minor	vital	

1. Not important: _____, _____, _____

2. Important: _____, _____, _____

3. Very important: _____, _____, _____

HOW DID YOU DO?

Once you have completed the chart, compare your responses with those of your classmates. Most students will probably list them as follows:

Not important: minor, insignificant, worthless

Important: serious, significant, notable

Very important: urgent, essential, vital

What other words can you think of that mean "very important"?

TYPES OF IMPORTANCE

Words that are related to importance can be confusing. One reason is that we have so many of them; another is that they sometimes differ from one another only slightly, and meanings overlap. Individual words related to the idea of importance can convey, or give, one of the following meanings:

- serious
- basic, core, or fundamental
- necessary, required

■ number one, or nearly so; first and foremost, primary

Remember that the context of the word tells its meaning, and the same word can sometimes have more than one meaning depending on its use.

Five useful words related to importance but that differ according to their use are *eminent, essential, momentous, paramount,* and *salient.* We'll look at each of these in turn.

Eminent

What meaning does *eminent* have in the following sentence? Does it indicate *"necessary"* or *"outstanding"*?

- Margaret Mead is *eminent* in the field of anthropology.

    Eminent means "having high standing," or "of high merit," or "distinguished." The term is often used with regard to scholars or individuals who have made significant contributions to science or the arts. Therefore, in this example *eminent* means "outstanding."

Essential

What meaning does *essential* have in the following sentence? Does it indicate "outstanding" or "necessary"?

- Teamwork was *essential* to the success of the project.

    Essential is related to the word *essence* and means "basic to the nature of something." In this case, the nature of the project required teamwork, so cooperation was *necessary.*

Momentous

What meaning does *momentous* have in the following sentence? Does it mean "serious" or "necessary"?

- Expanding the firm was a *momentous* decision for the directors.

    While the decision may well have been a necessary one, *momentous* means "serious," "weighty," or "major." *Momentous* is usually used to describe major decisions, issues, or events.

Paramount

What meaning does *paramount* have in the following sentence? Does it mean "serious" or "primary"?

- *Paramount* among the executive's concerns was that the company might lose money this year.

    Paramount indicates "first and foremost" or "primary." In this example, the concern about losing money was the *primary* concern. Losing money is also very *serious*, but we know that from our common sense, not from the word *paramount*.

Salient

What meaning does *salient* have in the following sentence? Does it mean "necessary" or "obvious"?

- The most *salient* point of the report was that the firm should employ ten more sales representatives.

    Salient means "obvious" or "standing out." To make its point salient, the report might have repeated the point, provided detail about it, presented it in larger print, or otherwise emphasized the need for added representatives. We do not know if the point was a foundation for the report, just that it was *obvious*. *Salient* does not usually refer to people; we say *salient* feature, point, response, issue, or observation, but not *salient* person, employee, or student.

WHAT DO YOU KNOW?

Circle the word in parentheses that best fits the phrase.

1. (essential / salient) step in the procedure
2. (paramount / eminent) issue
3. (momentous / eminent) physician
4. (eminent / salient) feature
5. (salient / momentous) decision

HOW DID YOU DO?

Answers: (1) essential; (2) paramount; (3) eminent; (4) salient; (5) momentous

Working with Words

WORD SELECTION

Circle the word in parentheses that best completes each sentence.

1. The purchase of the new equipment was _____ to the success of the firm. (momentous / essential / salient)

2. Their _____ concern was the health of their children. (paramount / eminent / essential)

3. The customers who attended the presentation were impressed with the _____ speaker. (momentous / essential / eminent)

4. The _____ feature of the product is the ease of use. (urgent / eminent / salient)

5. The firm's president was asked to speak at the _____ event. (salient / eminent / momentous)

FILL IN THE BLANKS

Write a word in the blank space provided that is "more than" the word given. Use words you already know . . . and your imagination!

Examples
louder than *talk*   *scream*
better than *good*   *excellent*

1. worse than *bad*   _____
2. thinner than *thin*   _____
3. older than *mature*   _____
4. younger than *adolescent*   _____
5. shinier than *bright*   _____
6. hotter than *warm*   _____
7. colder than *cool*   _____
8. wetter than *damp*   _____
9. madder than *angry*   _____
10. sadder than *blue*   _____

On a separate sheet of paper, write a sentence using each of the words you wrote in the blank spaces.

USING YOUR WORDS

Use each of the following phrases in a sentence that demonstrates that you understand the meaning of the phrase.

Example salient benefit
The salient benefit was the generous vacation time

1. the eminent physician

2. the salient feature

3. the essential part

4. a momentous occasion

5. the paramount concern

6. the salient point

7. essential to the formula

8. a momentous decision

9. eminent scholar

10. paramount achievement

Section 2 Review

The lessons in Section 2 addressed two goals: (1) to continue to build familiarity with a set of words for future understanding, use, and development; and (2) to examine relationships among words.

Lesson 7 presented words related to *communication*. Some of the ways that words related to communication can be grouped are as follows:

- two-way or one-way communication words (*exchange* or *tell*)
- sending or receiving words (*say* or *listen*; *imply* or *infer*)
- positive or negative communication words (*commend* or *admonish*)
- asking or answering words (*request* or *respond*)
- focused or wandering communication (*delineate* or *digress*)

Lesson 8 examined words related to *size* and *amount*. One way we looked at them was "in order"—in order of size and in order of amount. Words can indicate differences in *degree*—that is, one word can mean more or less of something than another word.

Words related to size and amount often occur in specific contexts. Words related to categories of small, large, many/much, enough, too many/too much, and few/little, with careful regard for their most common uses, were examined in this lesson.

In Lesson 9, we explored words related to the concept of *importance*. Words related to this concept express the order of importance through differences in meaning that may be slight but are significant. Types of importance that were identified included serious (*momentous*), basic or core (*essential*), necessary (*essential*), and primary (*eminent, paramount, salient*).

Working with Words

FIND THE MISFIT

In each group, underline the word that does not belong with the others. Then state why it doesn't belong.

1. praise, scold, ask, commend

2. listen, comprehend, understand, respond

3. imply, tell, apprise, comprehend

4. ramble, focus, wander, digress

5. apprise, assert, claim, comprehend

6. delineate, praise, state, inform

7. read, reply, refute, answer

8. infer, listen, imply, read

9. admit, confess, interrogate, tell

10. infer, interrogate, imply, inform

FILL IN THE BLANKS

From the following list, select the word that *best fits* the meaning of each sentence and write the word in the blank space provided. Use each word only once. Use all of the words. (*Hint:* First, complete the items you are sure of; then complete the more difficult ones.)

imply   infer   commend   admonish   digress   refute

1. I wish to _____ the mailroom staff for their efficient delivery system.
2. The manager did not directly state that the staff would receive a bonus, but she did _____ that they would.
3. George will _____ any employee who is not courteous to each and every customer.
4. The conference speaker had a tendency to _____. Consequently, her points were sometimes difficult to understand.
5. Am I to _____ from your lack of response that you do not wish to participate in this year's charity campaign?
6. He could not _____ the accusations made against him.

FIND THE ERROR

Each of the following sentences contains an error related to size or amount. Circle the word that is not used correctly, and write a word in the blank that better suits the sentence context.

_____ 1. Doug obtained the money for the copies from puny cash.

_____ 2. The report gave the financial information in miniature detail.

_____ 3. The developer borrowed money to construct the copious building.

_____ 4. The minute accounting clerk could not reach the invoices stored on the top shelf.

_____ 5. The financial statement did not show specific, diminutive amounts.

_____ 6. The marketing department prepared a spacious report on the potential for the new product.

_____ 7. The directors walked many hours touring the massive site for the new building complex.

_____ 8. The price of the new equipment was myriad, so the firm did not approve the purchase.

WORD GROUP ASSIGNMENTS

Make three groups of words from the following list. Each group should consist of three words that are most like each other. Use each word only once. Use all of the words.

abundant	ample	copious	diminutive	massive
spacious	petty	minute	myriad	

1. _____
2. _____
3. _____

WORD GROUP ASSIGNMENTS

Make five groups of words from the following list. Each group should consist of three words that are most like each other. Use each word only once. Use all of the words.

dearth	momentous	lack	massive	critical
urgent	paucity	enormous	heavy	insignificant
extravagant	petty	exorbitant	excessive	trivial

1. _____
2. _____
3. _____
4. _____
5. _____

WORD SELECTION

Circle the word in parentheses that best completes each sentence.

1. Because the machine operator forgot the _____ step of the process, the products were ruined. (essential / salient / momentous)

2. The _____ issue before the board of directors was whether to employ a consultant to solve the problem. (paramount / eminent / momentous)

3. The merger of the two firms was a _____ decision for the executives of both companies. (salient / momentous / eminent)

4. The _____ point made in the presentation was that many employee hours could be saved using the new system. (eminent / salient / momentous)

5. The board of trustees was composed of many _____ scholars and professionals. (momentous / eminent / urgent)

USING YOUR WORDS (REVIEW)

For each of the following words, write *either* a sentence using the word correctly *or* a brief explanation of its use.

1. apprise

2. imply

3. infer

4. commend

5. refute

6. digress

7. massive

8. puny

9. minute

10. trivial

11. petty

12. copious

13. extravagant

14. immoderate

15. meager

16. dearth

17. salient

18. paramount

19. essential

20. scold

Use each of the following phrases in a sentence that demonstrates that you understand the meaning of the phrase.

1. the eminent economist

2. the salient benefit

3. the essential ingredient

4. a momentous decision

5. the paramount issue

6. the salient feature

7. essential to the success

8. a momentous event

9. eminent physicist

10. paramount concern

Section 3
Word Analysis

Many English words are composites, or combinations, of several parts. *Prefixes* are letter groups that appear at the beginning of a word, before the root or base of the word. The *root* of a word is the main part. It contains the main part of the meaning. A *suffix* is a letter or letter group attached to the end of a root. Like prefixes, suffixes give us more information about the word. Knowing the meanings of prefixes and suffixes, together with the meanings of word bases or roots, will be particularly useful in understanding and learning to use new words. In Section 3 you will learn to recognize many common prefixes, roots, and suffixes. You will learn their meanings and how they combine to form different words.

Lessons 11 through 14 focus on prefixes. You will learn to recognize and use words with prefixes related to size, negation, amount, number, time, place, relationships, and judgments. Lessons 15 through 17 will teach you some of the roots used in English words. These include roots related to seeing, communicating, doing, and describing. Lessons 18 and 19 help you learn about suffixes, particularly suffixes that add meaning related to describing, doing, and naming.

WHAT DO YOU KNOW?

Write the meaning of each prefix, root, or suffix in the blank space provided. A word using each word part is provided as a hint. For more help, use a dictionary to check the meaning of the example word.

1. *un-, in-, im-* _____*not*_____ (unremarkable, inoperable, implausible)
2. *max-* _____ (maximum)
3. *min-* _____ (minimum)
4. *micro-* _____ (microphone)
5. *omni-* _____ (omnivorous)
6. *semi-* _____ (semiwild)
7. *hyper-* _____ (hyperactive)
8. *bi-* _____ (bisect)
9. *cent-* _____ (centipede)
10. *fore-* _____ (forewarn)
11. *ex-* _____ (exhale)
12. *peri-* _____ (perimeter)
13. *syn-* _____ (synthesize)
14. *bene-* _____ (benefit)
15. *-spect-, -vis-* _____ (perspective, visual)
16. *-dict-* _____ (dictator)
17. *-scrib-* _____ (transcribe)
18. *-lect-* _____ (lecture)
19. *-mit-* _____ (transmit)
20. *-mem-* _____ (remember)
21. *-ic* _____ (dramatic)
22. *-ize* _____ (characterize)
23. *-or* _____ (debtor)
24. *-ist* _____ (humorist)

HOW DID YOU DO?

(1) not; (2) most; (3) least; (4) small; (5) all; (6) half; (7) too much; (8) two; (9) hundred; (10) before; (11) out; (12) around; (13) together; (14) well; (15) see; (16) say/tell; (17) write; (18) read; (19) send; (20) mind; (21) characterized by; (22) to make or cause to be; (23), (24) doer

Prefixes

Size and Negation

Some prefixes change a word's meaning completely. For example, the prefix *un-* changes *able* to *unable*, and the prefix *non-* changes *sense* to *nonsense*. Sometimes a prefix alters the meaning by clarifying the word or making it more specific, such as *underground* or *aftertaste*. In this lesson, you will learn prefixes related to size and prefixes that mean "not."

PREFIXES RELATED TO SIZE

Some prefixes help define the size of something. Many of the words you worked with in Lesson 8 have prefixes. The prefixes *micro-* and *mini-* mean "small"; *macro-*, *magni-*, *maxi-*, and *mega-* all mean "large."

- To users of our customer service department *microcomputers:* To *maximize* your efficiency and *minimize* errors, please attend a seminar on using the *macro commands* that the information technology department has just programmed for us.
- He used a *microscope* to *magnify* the tissue so the germs could be identified.

The italicized terms in these statements have prefixes that mean "small" or "large."

Read the following examples and see if you know the meanings of the italicized prefixes.

micro- and mini-

microcomputer a small computer that uses a microchip or integrated circuit; includes PCs, Macs, and other types

microscope optical instrument for magnifying small objects

minimize reduce to the smallest size or quantity

macro-, magni-, maxi-, and mega-

macro command a long computer command made into abbreviated form; commonly referred to as a "macro"

magnify cause to appear larger

maximize enlarge to the greatest size or quantity

megabyte a million bytes (units of computer disk storage)

Other examples of words with these prefixes are *microcosm* ("a small universe"), *microphone*, *microfilm*, *minimum*, *magnitude*, *magnificent*, and *maximum*. (*Megalo-* is another prefix that means "large," as in *megalomania*.)

Mega has now entered our language as a common prefix to add before many terms to mean "very many," as in *megabucks*. In many cases, this usage is still colloquial, that is, casual or slang.

PREFIXES MEANING *NOT*

Some prefixes change the meaning of a word to its opposite. We call these *prefixes of negation* because they negate (make negative) the meaning. Some prefixes of negation are *non-*, *un-*, *in-*, *dis-*, *de-*, and *a-*. Understanding such words is not a difficult matter when you know the base word, or *root*. Knowing *which* prefix to use is a more complex problem. Following a few guidelines, listening and watching for words with prefixes in different contexts, and practicing will help you understand these words and use them properly.

non- and un-

- The machinery is *unusable* because it is *nonoperative*.
- The firm was penalized for *noncompliance* with safety regulations.
- That is a job for which Vera is *unqualified*.

Each italicized word in these statements can be restated using the word *not* with the base word. The machinery is *not usable* because it does *not operate*. The firm did *not comply* with the regulations. Vera is *not qualified* for the job.

non-   The meaning of this common prefix is seldom confused. *Non-* means *not*. *Nonsense* is clearly the opposite of *sense*. *Nonstandard* means, simply, "not standard." *Nonmetallic* means "not made of metal."

un-   *Un-*, like *non-*, can mean *not*. When *un-* is used with verbs, however, it gives the meaning of *reversal* of an action, as in *unlock* or *unchain*.

A few roots can combine with either *non-* or *un-* to form words that differ in meaning, such as *non-American* and *un-American*. How do these words differ in meaning? Which word means "lacking patriotism"? Which means "not of American origin, manufacture, or character"? The following examples will tell you.

- The spy gave secret government information to other countries; those actions were *un-American*.
- Our company does not buy products of *non-American* origin; they buy only goods made in the U.S.A.

nonproductive not productive; not producing

nonflammable not flammable

unambiguous not ambiguous or doubtful; clear, direct

uncover remove a covering

unsophisticated not sophisticated; simple

in- and *dis-*

- The firm's funds were *insufficient* to pay for a new computer.
- The *impartial* managers made an objective decision.
- That product is no longer available; its production has been *discontinued*.
- The sisters look alike, but their personalities are *dissimilar*.

Restate each of these sentences using a phrase with *not* to replace the italicized word. Also, try to think of a word to replace the italicized word that does not use a prefix meaning "not."

Insufficient can be stated as *not enough* (or *too little*); managers who are *impartial* are *not partial* or *not biased* (or *objective*); *discontinued* production is *not continued* (or *stopped*); and *dissimilar* is *not alike* (or *different*).

in-   One use of the prefix *in-* is to express negation. For example, *inaudible* means "not audible," or "not able to be heard." (The root comes from the Latin word *audire*, meaning "to hear.") *Indecisive* means "not decisive" or "not able to make a decision."

This prefix changes its spelling depending on the root or base word to which it is attached. Before *l*, *in-* becomes *il-*, as in *illogical* or *illegible*. Before *p* or *b* or *m*, *in-* becomes *im-*, as in *impossible*, *imbalance*, or *immature*. Before *r*, *in-* becomes *ir-*, as in *irregular* or *irresponsible*.

Some roots can combine with *non-* or *in-* to form words of different meanings. What is the difference between *nonhuman* and *inhuman*? Which word means "lacking human values and emotions"? Which means "not a human being"? Here they are in context:

- Their treatment of the prisoners was *inhuman*.
- The android was a *nonhuman* made to look like a human.

dis-   *Dis-* is another prefix used to convey a meaning of "not." The word *dishonest* means "not honest." *Dissimilar* means "not similar" or "different." What would *discontent* mean? In some words, *dis-* means "lack of." With verbs, *dis-* can indicate reversal, as in *disjoin* or *discontinue*.

The spelling of this prefix also changes. One common variation is *dif-*. The word *difficult*, for example, is formed by combining *dif-*, or "not," with a form of the Latin word *facilis*, which means "easy," giving us "not easy."

improbable not probable; unlikely   **disjoin** separate

ineligible not eligible   **discomfort** lack of ease

What are the meanings of the following prefixes?

1. *non-* _____
2. *un-* _____
3. *in-* _____
4. *dis-* _____

PREFIXES RELATED TO NEGATION

non-, un-, in-, dis- not

un-, dis- reversal of an action (used with verbs)

dis- lack of

A Note on *a-*

The prefix *a-* is complex and confusing. Sometimes *a-* means *not* or *without*. Common examples of this use are *atypical* and *absent*.

Other instances of the prefix *a-* mean *in, on,* or *at*, as in *asleep* or *aboard*.

Yet another form of *a-* means *up, on,* or *away*, as in *arise*.

Also, *a-* can mean *of* or *from*, as in *akin*.

As if things weren't complicated enough already, different forms or spellings of this prefix abound. *An-, ad-,* and *ab-* all abbreviate to *a*—and their spelling changes when combined with different letters! Generally, the *ab-* prefix indicates *off, from,* or *away; an-* indicates *not;* and *ad-* indicates *to-,* or *toward*.

For now, remember a few examples of words with the *a-* ("not") prefix: *atypical, amoral, aseptic,* and *amorphous*. These mean, respectively, "not typical," "not moral," "not infected," and "not having form or body."

Working with Words

FILL IN THE BLANKS

From the following list, select the word that best completes each sentence and write the word in the blank space provided. Use your knowledge of prefixes and context clues to help you decide. Use each word only once. Use all of the words.

minimum	ineligible	maximize	unambiguous
dishonest	minimize	microscope	nonproductive

1. Employees must work a _____ of one weekend per month.
2. The manager's statement was _____; she was very clear about her decision.
3. Employees and relatives are _____ for the store drawing.
4. We hope to _____ losses with our new inventory tracker.
5. The _____ salesperson made false claims about the product.
6. Our lab will examine the cells under a high-powered _____.
7. Without an agenda, our meeting will be _____.
8. The firm improved its efficiency, hoping to _____ its profits.

WORD COMPLETION

Complete each word in the left-hand column by adding one of the following prefixes. The meaning of the completed word is shown in the right-hand column.

mega-   in-   macro-   micro-   un-   dis-

1. _____ belief   not believing
2. _____ sophisticated   simple
3. _____ sufficient   not enough
4. _____ phone   voice amplifier
5. _____ scope   device that magnifies small objects
6. _____ command   long computer command

MULTIPLE CHOICE

Circle the letter next to the answer that best defines the italicized word. Some of these words have not been introduced previously; you will need to analyze context and word elements and use your knowledge of prefixes.

1. The invention was an *unsophisticated* machine that even a child could operate.

(a) simple   (c) complex

(b) fun   (d) sturdy

2. The doctor prescribed a *megadose* of antibiotics to treat her illness.
   - (a) number
   - (b) large amount
   - (c) variety
   - (d) small amount

3. We will not *disclose* the selling price until the contract is signed.
   - (a) advertise
   - (b) make public
   - (c) increase
   - (d) decrease

4. A helpful attitude can *disarm* an unhappy customer.
   - (a) anger
   - (b) win over
   - (c) upset
   - (d) amuse

5. The meeting was *atypical;* the president was absent.
   - (a) written
   - (b) typecast
   - (c) cheerful
   - (d) different

6. We need a *nonpartisan* chairperson to bring the two sides together.
   - (a) social
   - (b) free from anxiety
   - (c) respected
   - (d) objective

7. The *magnitude* of your decision, with so many jobs at stake, must be overwhelming.
   - (a) importance
   - (b) process
   - (c) basis
   - (d) result

8. The manager was *noncommittal* about the amount of the pay increases.
   - (a) vague
   - (b) angry
   - (c) generous
   - (d) direct

USING YOUR WORDS

Use each of the following words in a sentence that demonstrates that you understand the meaning of the word.

1. minimize

2. maximize

3. uncover

4. improbable

5. insufficient

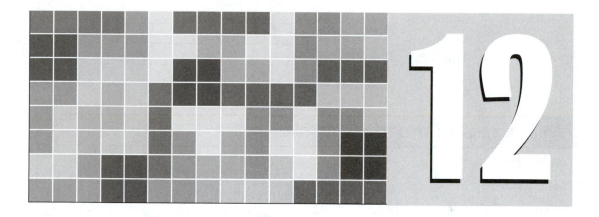

Prefixes

Amount and Number

PREFIXES RELATED TO AMOUNT OR EXTENT

All or Some

Some prefixes indicate an amount or a general idea of "how many." Read the following examples and see if you know the meanings of the italicized prefixes.

- The taxpayers paid for the *multi*million-dollar *poly*technic college that would prepare students in many arts.
- The decision to build a *Pan*-American highway from Canada to South America was *multi*lateral, or many sided. The entire Western *Hemi*sphere stands to benefit from this road.
- She is not vegetarian, but *omni*vorous.
- The president is *semi*retired and has time to watch the *semi*finals of the tennis tournament.

Based on these examples, what do the following prefixes mean?

multi-, poly-   _____

omni-, pan-   _____

semi-   _____

hemi-   _____

PREFIXES RELATED TO *ALL* OR *SOME*
multi-, poly- many
omni-, pan- all
semi- partial or half
hemi- half

Too Much

Some prefixes describe a large amount or extent of qualities. Read the following examples and see if you know the meanings of the italicized prefixes.

over-, hyper-, extra-, ultra-, and *super-*

*over*qualified having more training than required

*over*zealous excessively eager

*hyper*active medical condition producing extreme activity

*hyper*critical overly judgmental

*extra*ordinary beyond the normal; exceptional

*extra*vagant excessive expenditure; wasteful

*ultra*modern extremely modern or futuristic

*super*heat heat to excess; overheat

*super*fluous excessive; more than is needed

Based on these examples, what do the following prefixes mean?

over-   _____

hyper-   _____

extra-   _____

ultra-   _____

super-   _____

PREFIXES RELATED TO EXTENT
Over-, hyper-, extra-, ultra- too much, too many, extreme
Super- extra, excessive (In some cases, *super-* means "positioned above," as in *superimposed*.)

Too Little

Some prefixes describe a small amount or extent of qualities. Read the following examples and see if you know the meanings of the italicized prefixes.

hypo- and **under-**

hypothesis a theory requiring additional evidence

hypothermia condition marked by lowered body temperature

underfinanced lacking enough funding

underage not of a required age

underpay pay insufficiently

Based on these examples, what do the following prefixes mean?

hypo-   _____

under-   _____

MORE PREFIXES RELATED TO EXTENT
Hypo- too little, lacking
Under- too little, lacking (In some cases, *under-* means "positioned below," as in *underground*. See Lesson 13.)

PREFIXES EXPRESSING NUMBER

· Some words indicate very plainly a *number* of something, or "how many." One-way traffic moves in a single direction. A two-edged knife is sharp on both edges. A three-layer cake is, as it is named, a cake consisting of three layers. Many words indicate a number of something by using a prefix. You probably already know many words indicating numbers.

Ones

Fill in each blank space with the correct prefix.

1. A _____ corn is a fictional, horselike animal with one horn.
2. To _____ fy is to bring together or combine into a single unit.
3. The speaker gave her _____ logue at noon; the talk was _____ tonous.
4. Plans for the new rapid transportation system include building a _____ rail.

Did you write *unicorn, unify, monologue, monotonous,* and *monorail*? The prefixes *uni-* and *mono-* mean "single" or "one."

Twos

Now insert prefixes that mean "two."

1. Elena speaks English and Spanish. She is _____ lingual.
2. That agreement was _____ lateral. Both sides were party to it.
3. That music is a _____ et for piano and violin.
4. We need two copies; please submit your offer in _____ plicate.
5. They meet every two years. This _____ ennial event is well attended.

Did you write *bilingual, bilateral, duet, duplicate,* and *biennial? Bi-* and *du-* are prefixes that mean "two."

Less common are the prefixes *di-* and *diplo-.* We see *di-* in science, as in *dioxide* ("having two oxygen atoms"). A *diplomat* is one who deals with others; the word comes from the history of the diplomat as someone who delivers or exchanges letters, letters folded in two, or doubled.

Threes

Now try some prefixes that mean "three."

1. The form has three sheets alike. It is in _____ plicate.
2. Ken has not mastered his bicycle. He still rides his _____ cycle.

3. A closed figure with three sides enclosing three angles is a _____ angle.

Did you write *tri-* in all three blank spaces to indicate "three"?

PREFIXES RELATED TO ONE, TWO, AND THREE
mon-, mono, uni- one
bi-, di-, diplo-, du- two
tri- three

Tens, Hundreds, and Thousands

Write a prefix in each blank space. If you are not sure of the prefix, refer to the following box.

1. The 1960s were the _____ ade of the "flower children."
2. A decade is one-tenth of a _____ ury.
3. In 1976, the United States celebrated the bi _____ ennial of its independence.
4. A _____ ipede has many legs, but maybe not exactly 100.
5. The speedometer on his car shows its speed in miles as well as in _____ meters.
6. That personal computer has 512 _____ bytes (or 512,000 bytes) of RAM.
7. A _____ ennium is a period of 1,000 years.
8. One _____ on is equal to one thousand thousand, or 1,000,000.

PREFIXES RELATED TO TENS
deca- ten
cent- hundred
milli-, kilo- thousand

Working with Words

WORD REPLACEMENT

The following memo contains underlined phrases that could be stated as single words. Find the word in the following list that suits the definition and sentence context of each phrase, and write it in the corresponding blank space provided. You will not use all of the words.

overpriced	ultramodern	multiple	decade
hypercritical	multimillion	extraordinary	biweekly

Memorandum

TO: Sales Staff

FROM: Wayne Ryan, Marketing Director

SUBJECT: Customer Survey

DATE: March 5, 200X

Our marketing department recently conducted a survey of credit card customers to get their reaction to the (1) <u>more-than-one-million-dollar</u> expansion of Bob's Department Store. Our customers were very cooperative in answering our questions, although a few were (2) <u>overly judgmental</u> about some of Bob's services. The survey reveals that most of our customers believe Bob's products are (3) <u>far too expensive</u>. The majority believe that the new (4) <u>very futuristic</u> store is (5) <u>highly exceptional</u>, and they enjoy the surroundings.

   A profile of our shoppers shows that most have been loyal to us for over (6) <u>ten years</u> and shop at our store (7) <u>every two weeks</u>.

Many customers own (8) <u>more than one</u> charge card and shop at both stores.

1. _____

2. _____

3. _____

4. _____

5. _____

6. _____

7. _____

8. _____

FIND THE MATCH

Circle the word that is closest in meaning to each italicized word.

1. *extraordinary*: simple, truthful, remarkable
2. *overjoyed*: bored, ecstatic, placid
3. *omnipresent*: vanished, everywhere, nowhere
4. *multiply*: increase, engage, equate
5. *hypothesis*: experiment, theory, novel
6. *underprivileged*: supported, unhappy, deprived

WORD SELECTION

Circle the word in parentheses that best completes each sentence.

1. Please form a _____ with your chairs to facilitate group discussion. (semi-circle / hemisphere)
2. Unfortunately, management believed that the candidate was _____ and would soon become bored. (overqualified / extraordinary)
3. A _____ is more than a decade. (century / millisecond)
4. Ignore the _____ details and just focus on the main problem. (extraneous / dichotomous)
5. Since all three departments need the document, I'll have it reproduced in _____. (triplicate / duplicate)
6. Their efforts to slow us down were simply intended to _____ our newest advertising campaign. (superheat / undermine)

7. Those animals are _____; they eat both animal and vegetable foods. (omnivorous / omnipresent)

8. A thousand thousand is one _____. (million / trillion)

TRUE OR FALSE?

Circle T or F to indicate whether each of the following statements is true or false. Use the sentence context and your knowledge of prefixes to help you decide.

T F   1. A kilometer is less than a *centimeter*.

T F   2. Someone who is *hypersensitive* to a particular food should not eat it.

T F   3. A *bifocal* lens contains two corrections in one lens.

T F   4. *Pandemonium* means "demons everywhere."

T F   5. A *bilateral* agreement is one made by three committees.

T F   6. A *bilingual* person is someone who speaks two languages.

T F   7. You probably work part time if you are *semiretired*.

T F   8. A *monologue* is a script of a conversation.

T F   9. A *unicorn* and a rhinoceros might be related.

T F 10. A *hypothermal* blanket is very warm.

USING YOUR WORDS

Use each of the following words in a sentence that demonstrates that you understand the meaning of the word.

1. multicolored

2. superfluous

3. unify

4. bilingual

5. triplicate

Prefixes

Time and Place

PREFIXES EXPRESSING TIME

Prefixes related to time tell you when something happened or will happen. You will learn to recognize prefixes related to *before*, *after*, and *again* and to use words containing these prefixes. How many words can you find in the following letter that have a prefix meaning "after" or "later"? Which have a prefix that means "before"? Which have a prefix meaning "again"? Circle the words with those prefixes. You will be surprised at how many English words use these prefixes.

Dear Mr. Johnson:

I am very pleased that our appointment was not postponed

and that we will be able to meet Tuesday afternoon.

Foremost on our list of issues to discuss is the need

to forewarn your employees about the firm's intention to

```
renovate the building and that they should take

precautions to protect their clothing before visiting

any work area. A little foresight will help prevent any

recurrence of the problems we had with building repairs

last year. Our building committee chairwoman reiterated

the importance of preparing everyone for the

inconvenience.
```

Did you circle *postponed, afternoon, foremost, forewarn, renovate, precautions, protect, foresight, prevent, recurrence, repairs, reiterated,* and *preparing?*

post-, after-

Did you find *postponed* and *afternoon? Post-* indicates "later" or "after." A *postscript* is something added after a letter has been completed; to *postdate* a check or other document is to date it *after* the actual date—that is, some date in the future. *After-* is a common prefix. *Afternoon* means "sometime between noon and sunset"; an *aftertaste* is a taste that is sensed after something is swallowed; an *afterthought* is an idea that occurs after the main thinking, discussion, or event.

fore-, pre-, pro-, ante-

Did you find *foremost, forewarn, foresight,* and *precautions?* Both *fore-* and *pre-* indicate a time or occurrence *before* or *first. Foremost* means "first in importance" or "before others." To *forewarn* is to warn in advance; *foresight* is the ability to look forward. A *precaution* is something done beforehand to avoid harm; to *prevent* is also to do something before an occurrence in order to stop it; to *prepare* is to get something ready; and a *prefix* is attached (or "fixed") ahead of something, like a word root.

Two other prefixes that indicate "before" are *pro-* and *ante-. Pro-* is seen in words such as *prologue,* an introductory statement, or *prognosis,* a prediction of the course of an illness. To *protect* means "to defend from possible (future) harm," or literally, "to cover beforehand." *Ante-* is the prefix in *antedate,* which means "precede" or "date something before the actual date." An *anteroom* is a waiting room. *Antecedent* means "something prior or preceding": Her bad attitude was *antecedent to* (before) the termination of her job.

re-

The sample letter also contained words with the prefix *re-*, meaning "again." *Renovate* means "make new again or renew"; *reiterate* means "state again." What does the context of the letter and analysis of the word *recurrence* tell you about its meaning?

PREFIXES RELATED TO TIME
post-, after- later or after
fore-, pre-, pro-, ante- something that occurs before or first
re- again (*Re-* can also mean "back," as in *remit*, "send back." See the next section in this lesson.)

PREFIXES RELATED TO PLACE

A number of prefixes indicate place or direction; they tell us *where*. These prefixes indicate *in* or *out; to* or *from; around, across,* or *through; above* or *below*. You are probably familiar with a great many words that use these prefixes.

How many words can you find in the following paragraph that have a prefix meaning "around," "across," or "through"? Which have a prefix meaning "over" or "under"? "Into" or "out of"? Circle the words with those prefixes.

> The ship arrived in the harbor after a year at sea with the crew looking tired and worn. They had circumnavigated the globe; it had taken them more than a year. Still no rest was in sight. The cargo had to be transferred from the interior of the ship to the warehouse. Papers had to be filled out and submitted to the customs officer for everything being imported to this city and then for the exports that would be loaded into the hold, bound for other parts of the world. All the permits had to be in order before the goods could be loaded. Then the crew could go into the town. But Hector reclined on his bunk, book in hand. . . .

Did you circle *circumnavigated, transferred, interior, submitted, imported, exports, permits,* and *reclined?* The prefixes of these words are discussed in the following sections. Make a list of five (or more) other words with these prefixes that indicate "where."

super - and *sub* -; *over* - and *under* -

Super- and sub- mean "above" and "below," respectively. To *supervise* means, literally, "oversee." *Subterranean* is formed from the prefix meaning "under" and the base *terra*, meaning "earth," giving us "underground."

We saw *over-* and under- in the previous lesson, meaning "too much" or "too little." In some cases these prefixes related to place rather than amount. In both *overhead* and *overhand*, the prefix refers to a location above. In *underline* and *underground*, the prefix refers to a location below.

ex - and *im* - or *in* -; *intro* - and *extra* -

Ex- and im- are prefixes meaning "out" and "in." To *export* is to send something out of the country, or "from the port." What is *import*? *Exhale* and *inhale* refer to breathing out and in. If *-hibit* is a word base or root meaning "hold," what are *exhibit* and *inhibit*? *Explain* combines a base meaning "level" with *ex-*, giving us "level out or make plain or understandable."

Intro- and *extro-* or *extra-* are related prefixes, meaning "inside" and "outside." The terms *introvert* and *extrovert* are examples; if *-vert* refers to "turning," what do these terms mean? To *introduce* is to "lead into" something. Do you know the meanings of *extraterrestrial* and *extracurricular*?

inter -

The prefix *inter-* means "among" or "between." For example, to *intercede* is to "go between" two parties. To *interrupt* is to "break into" a conversation or activity. Do you see this prefix in *internal* and *interior*?

per -

The prefix *per-* means *thorough*, *throughout*, or *through*. For example, to be *perfect* is to be thoroughly correct, to "carry it through." To *perceive* is to "be totally aware of something." *Permanent* combines the prefix *per-* with a root that means "remain," giving us something that continues without change.

trans -

Trans- means "across." To *transcend* means to "go across." *Transfer* is based on the root meaning "carry," giving us "carry across." When we *transfer* money from a savings account to a checking account, it is "carried across" from one account to the other.

circum – and *peri –*

Circum- and *peri-* both mean "around." To *circumvent* means to come around an obstacle or problem. To *circumnavigate* the globe means to sail around it. In some instances this prefix drops its *m* (as in the word *circulate*, meaning "pass around") or drops its *-um* ending (as in the word *circle*).

Periscope combines *peri-* with *scope*, which means "look," giving us something that helps us "look around" an object. *Perimeter* includes the root *meter*, which comes from a word meaning "to measure." The *perimeter* of an area is the measurement around it.

re – and *retro –*

We saw *re-* in the previous section in this lesson with words that use it in the sense of "again." *Re-* can also mean "back," as does *retro-*. *Recline* combines *re-* with a root that means "to lean," giving us the meaning "lean back." *Retroactive* means "acting back in time" or "becoming effective some time in the past." *Retrospect* combines *retro-* with a root, *-spect-*, meaning "look"—providing us with a word that means "looking back in time." To *retrofit* is to provide newly designed parts for an existing piece of machinery.

REMINDERS

What does each of the following prefixes mean? For each one, write the meaning and a word that uses the prefix. Try to use examples that have not been used previously.

	MEANING	EXAMPLE
ante-		
circum-		
ex-		
inter-		
intro-		
pre-		
per-		
post-		
re-		
re-		
retro-		
trans-		

PREFIXES RELATED TO PLACE

super-, over- above

sub-, under- below

ex- from

in-, im- in, into

intro- inside

extro- outside

per- throughout

trans- across

circum-, peri- around

re-, retro- back

Working with Words

FILL IN THE BLANKS

From the following list, select the prefix that best completes each word and write the prefix in the blank space provided. The root of the word is provided for you. Use the sentence context to help you decide. Some prefixes will be used more than once, but use all of them.

fore-   pro-   ex-   trans-
intro-   circum-   pre-   per-

In the (1) _____ logue that (2) _____ duces his book, *The Computer User at Work,* author Kenneth Harms (3) _____ plains the (4) _____ stances under which he decided to write about computers in the workplace. Several years ago, Harms noticed that computer usage (5) _____ vaded all the departments in his company. Harms decided that he needed to learn how to operate a computer soon—or risk the loss of his job. *The Computer User at Work* is intended to help readers learn to (6) _____ form some basic computer operations. Harms (7) _____ lates computer jargon for the nonuser and (8) _____ duces concepts in simple form. If you (9) _____ see computers entering your workplace, I highly recommend that you (10) _____ pare yourself by reading this book.

MULTIPLE CHOICE

Circle the letter next to the sentence that best explains the numbered statement.

1. The town had no forewarning of the earthquake.
    (a) The town was destroyed.
    (b) The town was frightened.
    (c) The earthquake never happened.
    (d) The town was taken by surprise.

2. The firm postdated the check to the following Monday.
    (a) The check was dated after it was cashed.
    (b) The check was blank until Monday.
    (c) The check was not valid until the next Monday.
    (d) There was no money in the bank account.

3. The clerk transferred the funds to another account.
   (a) The clerk ran away with the money.
   (b) Money was moved from one account to another.
   (c) There was no money.
   (d) The clerk was dishonest.

4. The sales clerk set up the book exhibit.
   (a) The clerk made appointments for authors.
   (b) The clerk put books on display.
   (c) The books were on sale.
   (d) The exhibit was a failure.

5. June's pay increase was retroactive six months.
   (a) The firm delayed giving pay increases.
   (b) June had to wait six months before receiving a raise.
   (c) The increase was made effective for the six previous months.
   (d) The pay increase blew up.

6. Harry makes a good salesman; he is a real extrovert.
   (a) Harry talks too much.
   (b) Harry is outgoing.
   (c) Harry is a "smooth talker."
   (d) Harry understands people.

USING YOUR WORDS

Use each of the following words in a sentence that demonstrates that you understand the meaning of the word.

1. postpone

2. forewarn

3. supervise

4. transfer

5. export

Prefixes

Relationships and Judgment

PREFIXES EXPRESSING RELATIONSHIPS

Some prefixes express a relationship when attached to a root word.

Read the following excerpt and circle the words that you think have a prefix that means "with" or "together."

> In order to complete the committee's report on the equipment problems, the members will need to collaborate. Max is corresponding with the manufacturer, but the manufacturer is not being very cooperative. While the company is sympathetic, it refuses to replace the machines. The committee might conclude that it should replace the machinery with new equipment from another source. We are confident that, whatever the outcome, the equipment will be ready to make the new synthetic fabrics next month.

Did you circle *committee, collaborate, corresponding, cooperative, sympathetic, conclude,* and *synthetic*? All of these words begin with a prefix that means "with" or "together."

com-

Com- and its various spellings (co-, cor-, col-, and con-) means "together" or "with." *Committee* combines com- with a root we have seen before, -mit-, meaning "to send." A committee is, therefore, a group of people sent together to report or act on a matter.

Before *l*, the prefix becomes col-, as in *collaborate*, which combines the prefix with a root meaning of labor or work, giving us "work together."

Before *r*, the prefix becomes cor-, as in *correspond*, or "responding to one another."

Con- is a spelling of this prefix that is used before many consonants (*c*, *d*, *f*, *g*, *j*, *n*, *q*, *s*, *t*, *v*), as in *conclude*, or "end together" or "bring together in the end."

Cooperate uses the co- spelling of the prefix to give us "operate together." We see this spelling before vowels. Based on this information, how would you define *coordinate*? (The root is from the Latin word *ordinare*, meaning "to put in order.")

syn-

The prefix syn-, also spelled sym- and syl-, means "together." *Synthetic* combines the prefix with a root that means "to place or put"; something that is *synthetic* has been made by putting things together. To *synchronize*, which combines the root -chron-, meaning "time," means to "occur at the same time" or to "operate in unison."

Sympathy combines the sym- form of the prefix with a root that means "feeling," giving us "feeling together" or "sharing feelings."

A word that uses syl- is *syllable*, a set of letters (or "labels") taken together and voiced in a single impulse or spurt.

PREFIXES EXPRESSING A JUDGMENT

Some prefixes qualify or express a judgment about the root to which they are attached.

bene-, mal-, and mis-

Which terms in the following sentences mean something good? Which mean something bad?

* The firm provides its employees a very good *benefits* package.
* Exercise and a wholesome diet are *beneficial* to one's health.

- The test showed that the growth was not *malignant*.
- The *benevolent* gentleman made a generous donation to their group.
- Her *misfortune* saddened everyone around her.

The prefix *bene-* comes to us from the Latin for "well" or "good." *Benefit* and the related adjective *beneficial* combine this prefix with a form of the Latin word *facere*, meaning "to do," giving us something that is helpful. *Benevolent* joins this prefix with a root that means "will" or "wish," so *benevolence* is good will.

The prefix *mal-* is from a Latin word meaning "bad." In contrast to *benevolence*, *malevolence* is ill will. Likewise, *malignant* means "evil" or "ill-disposed." A *malignant* tumor is one that does great harm. To *malfunction* is to function poorly or break down.

Like *mal-*, *mis-* indicates "bad" or "amiss." *Misfortune* is, therefore, bad luck. And a *mishap* is an accident or unfortunate happening.

Working with Words

TRUE OR FALSE?

Circle T or F to indicate whether each of the following statements is true or false.

T F   1. A benefit indicates how well a suit fits.

T F   2. Someone who coordinates an event puts it together so it runs smoothly.

T F   3. To be sympathetic is to find a good path to solve a problem.

T F   4. Nylon is a synthetic fabric.

T F   5. If we collaborate on a project, we do it together.

T F   6. If our answers to the questions are consistent, they are opposite from one another.

T F   7. If we are cooperating, we are building a house for chickens.

T F   8. If your computer malfunctions, you may need to call in a repairperson.

T F   9. An evil being, such as a witch, is often considered to be malevolent.

T F 10. Cigarette smoking is beneficial to your health.

FIND THE MISFIT

In each group, underline the word that does not belong with the others. Then state why it doesn't belong.

1. healthy, beneficial, good, facial

2. malignant, evil, ligature, wicked

3. close, conclude, rude, end

4. pity, sympathy, road, feeling

5. combination, synthetic, synchronize, beneficial

6. time, synchronize, sinful, coincide

MULTIPLE CHOICE

Circle the letter next to the answer that best defines the italicized word or phrase. Use your knowledge of prefixes to help you decide.

1. She is still recovering from the *malady.*
   (a) opera
   (b) illness
   (c) occurrence
   (d) happening

2. Those plays represent the author's *compassionate* view of life.
   (a) sympathetic
   (b) directional
   (c) passing
   (d) fatalistic

3. His grandparents do not understand his like of *contemporary* music.
   (a) fast
   (b) loud
   (c) current
   (d) bad

4. Everyone *congregated* in the auditorium during the storm.
   (a) talked
   (b) gathered together
   (c) worried
   (d) ate

5. The *consensus* of everyone who attended the play was that it was too long.
   (a) decision
   (b) frustration
   (c) collective opinion
   (d) permission

6. The physician was sued for *malpractice.*
   (a) operating on a dog
   (b) practicing music
   (c) giving improper or injurious treatment
   (d) not paying a hospital bill

7. The professor prepared the course *syllabus.*
   (a) concise overview or outline of main points
   (b) vehicle for a course field trip
   (c) test
   (d) classroom

8. We enjoyed our trip to the music center to hear the *symphony.*
   (a) percussion instruments
   (b) concert
   (c) speaker
   (d) amplifiers

Roots

Seeing and Communicating

English is based on Anglo-Saxon with strong influences from Latin, because Latin was the language of the Romans, who conquered Britain. English has borrowed many words or parts of words. These influences and borrowings help explain why we often have several different words that have very similar meanings. In this sense, our language is an extremely rich one.

Roots have been mentioned in previous lessons as the "core" of a word. The root of a word is its heart, before the addition of a prefix to the beginning or a suffix to the end of the word.

You will see that some roots have more than one form, and the differences are reflected in our English words as well. *Commit* and *commission* are related words: *Commit* is the verb (as in "to commit a crime") and *commission* is the noun (as in "commission of a crime"). *Transmit* and *transmission, permit* and *permission,* all have the same root meaning "to send." The spelling of the root changes from *-mit-* to *-mis-* for some words.

Remember that our language has gone through many changes, and often we recognize the root, prefixes, and suffixes, but still the meaning of the term as it is used today is not clear. (The history of words and the changes they have undergone take up an entire branch of study known as *etymology.*) Nonetheless, familiarity with Latin and Greek roots, as well as with prefixes and suffixes, will provide you with a significant advantage when determining the meaning of unfamiliar words and phrases.

SEEING ROOTS

This lesson introduces some common Latin and Greek roots. The first of these are related to seeing. Which of the words in the following description are related to seeing? Circle the words that you think might have roots related to seeing. Then read the remainder of the lesson to see if you identified them all.

> The inspector inspected the telescope carefully. "Unless my vision needs to be checked," he thought, "these fingerprints belong to the most evil criminal in the land. I suspect that I finally have evidence of the crime. I'll need to visit the lab to put these fingerprints under the microscope."

Did you circle *inspector, inspected, telescope, vision, suspect, evidence, vision,* and *microscope?*

-scop-

This root comes from a Greek word that means "to look at." We usually find it in English nouns and adjectives, but seldom in verbs. Some words with this root are *scope, microscope, telescope, periscope, stethoscope,* and related adjectives and adverbs such as *microscopic* and *telescopically.*

The Greek word for chest is *stethos.* What apparatus helps us "see" into a person's chest?

-spect-, -spectr-

The root *-spect-* comes from the Latin root meaning "to look at." Our words *inspect, suspect, respect, perspective, circumspect, spectator,* and *spectacle* are examples of English words with this root. *Circum-* is a prefix you learned in a previous lesson meaning "around." *Circumspect* means "cautious" or "watchful" or "attentive to detail." Can you think of other words with this root?

The *-spectr-* form of this root gives us the English words *spectrum,* which is a "visible band of color," and *specter,* which is a "ghost or apparition."

-vid-, -vis-

Latin also gives us the root *-vid-* and the related *-vis-.* Both of these are forms of the same origin, "to see." Our English word *video* is actually the Latin word for "I see." The word *evidence* is based on this root.

We use the *-vis-* form in *vision* and *visionary, revision* and *revisionist.* A *vista* is a wide view, and to *visit* is to see someone. *Visual* pertains to the sense of sight, and to *visualize* is to form a mental image.

COMMUNICATING ROOTS

Several roots are related to words we use about communicating: stating, writing, questioning, and reading. Which of the words in the following description are related to these aspects of communicating? Circle the parts of the words that you think might have "communicating" roots. Then read the remainder of the lesson to see if you found them all.

> The attorney scribbled a list of questions to be asked at the inquest. She was sure that a description of the crime scene would be requested, and a copy of the drug prescription, and probably a transcript of the confession. Her notes were barely legible, but she would dictate them later for the clerk to transcribe.

> Did you circle *scribbled, questions, inquest, description, requested, prescription, transcript, legible, dictate,* and *transcribe?*

-dict-

English obtained the root *-dict-* from the Latin word meaning "to say." English combines this root with the prefix *ver-,* which means "true," to give us a word that means a judgment or decision of a jury: *verdict.* One's *diction* is how one speaks, and a *dictionary* gives us words, their definitions, and pronunciations. When we *dictate,* we speak aloud or command. *Edict, contradict,* and *predict* all combine this root with a prefix to form different English words.

-scrib-, -script-

While *scribbling* is done in haste and carelessly, or sometimes by children imitating the writing process, the word itself has an honorable origin, coming from the Latin word *scribere* meaning "to write." The word *scribe* and its many combination forms, such as *describe, prescribe,* and *subscribe,* are other words using this root.

When combined words are changed to form nouns, we see the *-script-* forms *description, prescription, subscription, inscription,* and the word *script* itself. Review the following definitions of *-script-* words.

subscription a promise to pay (signature at the end of an agreement, or "write under"), often for issues of a newspaper or magazine. (What is the cost of a *subscription* to that paper?)

prescription a written order or direction, as for a medicine or treatment. (Did you pick up the *prescription* at the pharmacy?)

description a written or spoken picture; account. (She wrote a *description* of the accident.)

inscription words written in something, as a watch or ring. (The *inscription* on the trophy read "Best Player, 1992.")

script handwriting; also, a written document, such as a play. (He wrote a *script* for that television series.)

transcript a written (typewritten, word-processed) copy; also, academic record. (She sent her *transcript* from Stanford University.)

-leg-, -lect-

The two root forms *-leg-* and *-lect-* come to English from the Latin *legere*, "to read." The *-leg-* appears in *legible*, meaning "readable," and *illegible*, "not readable." *Lectures* were, at one time, read to an audience, although now lectures are sometimes given from notes, from memory, or spontaneously. Likewise, a *lectern* is a stand for a speaker's notes and books from which a lecture is read.

-quer-, -quest-

Query, *quest*, *inquest*, *request*, and *question* all have the root forms *-quer-* or *-quest-*, from the Latin word meaning "to ask." Another form of the root is *-quire-*, as in *inquire* and *require*. How is a *quest*, or search, a form of asking?

REMINDERS

Write the root of each word. Then write a definition of the word.

1. microscope
2. spectator
3. evidence
4. legible
5. inscription
6. question
7. visit
8. dictate

Working with Words

FILL IN THE BLANKS

From the following list, select the word that best completes each sentence and write the word in the blank space provided. Use your knowledge of roots to help you decide. Use each word only once. Use all of the words.

legible	requests	dictates	visit
inquiries	scribbling	microscope	prescriptions

Memorandum

TO: Hospital Staff

FROM: Administration Office

SUBJECT: Weekly Announcements

DATE: September 14, 200X

Several of you have received (1) _____ from patients'

relatives to (2) _____ outside of the official hours.

All special requests concerning visiting hours should be

referred to the hospital administrator. Most (3) _____

about general policies can be answered by consulting the new

manual. A copy is available at each station.

    Please pay extra attention to the filling of (4) _____.

While the handwriting of some physicians is not as

(5) _____ as we would like, their notes are not careless

(6) _____, but critical medical (7) _____.

Finally, we are pleased to announce that the hospital museum has

received a fine donation from Dr. Smith, a fine antique

(8) _____.

ROOT IDENTIFICATION

Circle the root of each word. Then write a definition of the word.

1. telescope

2. spectacles

3. visit

4. illegible

MULTIPLE CHOICE

Circle the letter next to the answer that best completes the sentence. Use your knowledge of contextual clues, prefixes, and roots to help you decide.

1. The organisms that attacked the patient's lungs were _____.
   (a) telescopic   (c) microscopic
   (b) visionary   (d) circumspect

2. The periscope could be extended several yards; it was _____.
   (a) telescopic   (c) microscopic
   (b) visionary   (d) circumspect

3. The firm was very _____ about revealing information about its new products before their formal introduction.
   (a) telescopic   (c) microscopic
   (b) evidential   (d) circumspect

4. The doctor gave her a _____ to help fight her cold.
   (a) transcription   (c) subscription
   (b) prescription   (d) inscription

5. I ordered a _____ to the *Harvard Business Review*.
  (a) transcription   (c) subscription
  (b) prescription   (d) inscription

6. What was the _____ on the watch?
  (a) transcription   (c) subscription
  (b) prescription   (d) inscription

7. Unfortunately, her handwriting was not _____.
  (a) telescopic   (c) legible
  (b) visible   (d) subscribed

8. The referee asked the _____ to be quiet.
  (a) inquirees   (c) spectators
  (b) dictators   (d) scribes

USING YOUR WORDS

Use each of the following words in a sentence that demonstrates that you understand the meaning of the word.

1. illegible

2. inscription

3. predict

4. circumspect

5. inspection

Roots

Doing

The roots that you will learn to recognize and use in this lesson are all related to doing or actions. Many English words are derived from these roots related to carrying, sending, and turning. Circle the words in the following passage that you think might have roots related to carrying, sending, or turning.

> The Arbor Imports Company has recently announced that a new conifer developed in the Orient is now available at its greenhouses for immediate transfer to your garden. This new tree, which Arbor imported by obtaining a special permit from the agricultural commission, is a garden miniature that grows to about three feet. Begin now to convert your yard to a serene retreat from worldly cares. Visit Arbor Imports today!

Did you circle *imports*, *conifer*, *transfer*, *permit*, *commission*, and *convert*?

-PORT-, -FER-

The Latin verb *portare*, meaning "to carry," gives us the root found in *portable*, *porter*, *deport*, *report*, *transport*, *import*, and *export*, among others.

Another Latin verb that means "to carry" or "to bring" is *ferre*. The *-fer-* root from this verb is found in *ferry*, *transfer*, *refer*, and others. An interesting noun that uses this root is *conifer*, a cone-bearing tree.

-MIT-, -MIS-

Several words with this root, from the Latin *mittere*, meaning "to send," were discussed in previous lessons. *Remit, submit, admit, commit, transmit, permit,* and *emit* have the root meaning "to send" as their base. Other forms of these verbs, particularly noun forms, use the *-mis-* form of the root: *remission, submission, admission,* and so on. A *missive* is a letter or other matter that is sent somewhere. Based on this information, how would you define a *missile?* What about *mission* and *intermission?*

-VERT-, -VERS-

-Vert- and the form we find in nouns, *-vers-,* come from the Latin word *vertere,* meaning "to turn." *Revert,* for example, means "turn back" or "return." Its noun forms are *reverse* and *reversion,* meaning "turned back."

Convertible is a term popularized by the automobile industry in the 1950s, although use of the word is far from being limited to autos. The term uses a meaning of the root *-vert-* that indicates "to change," and means "changeable."

Based on this information about the root *-vert-,* how might you explain the derivation of the words *vertical* and *versus?* Perhaps *vertical* developed through the concept of being turned on end, while *versus* could have developed from usage that indicated turned against, as in "the Angels versus the Twins."

REMINDERS

Circle the root of each word. Then write a definition of the word.

1. remit

2. consent

3. export

4. introvert

5. intermission

6. transfer

Working with Words

MULTIPLE CHOICE

Circle the letter next to the answer that best defines the italicized word. Use your knowledge of contextual clues, prefixes, and roots to help you decide.

1. Please *transfer* the funds from my checking account to my savings account.
   (a) move
   (b) cross
   (c) subtract
   (d) bear

2. He received the *missive* about his new job by overnight mail.
   (a) gun
   (b) application
   (c) letter
   (d) news

3. Please *convert* these Mexican pesos to dollars.
   (a) add
   (b) permit
   (c) revert
   (d) change

4. Please *remit* payment for the invoice in the preaddressed envelope.
   (a) send
   (b) exchange
   (c) revert
   (d) apply

5. How will the goods be *transferred* to the warehouse?
   (a) moved to
   (b) billed to
   (c) kept at
   (d) refrigerated at

6. They used an old shortwave radio to *transmit* the message.
   (a) get
   (b) change
   (c) send
   (d) shorten

7. Please deliver that *portable* computer to our other office.
   (a) up-to-date
   (b) easy-to-carry
   (c) door-opening
   (d) waterproof

8. Be sure that the fence posts are *vertical*.
   (a) exactly upright
   (b) flat
   (c) even
   (d) deep

USING YOUR WORDS

Circle the root of each word. Then use each word in a sentence that demonstrates that you understand the meaning of the word.

1. transport

2. remit

3. transfer

4. convert

5. portable

6. transmission

7. ferry

8. vertical

9. export

10. emit (*Hint:* The prefix *e-* is a form of *-ex-*, or "out.")

Roots

Describing

Like the action words presented in Lesson 16, some words that describe people, places, and things have their basis in roots borrowed from Latin and Greek. In this lesson, you will learn to recognize and use roots related to describing time, change, being sure, truth, and finality.

-CERT-

What do the words containing the root *-cert-* in the following sentences mean?

- I am *certain* that he is mistaken.
- I *certify* that this is correct.
- Please send a *certified* check to pay that invoice.
- We need a copy of your birth *certificate*.
- Please *ascertain* the whereabouts of the suspect on June 3.

The root *-cert-* comes from the Latin word *cernere*, which means "to determine." Used in English derivatives, the root means "sure" or "confident."

-MEM-

What do the words containing the root *-mem-* in the following sentences mean?

- Do you *remember* the phone number for the bank?
- He has a great *memory*; he remembers conversations from years ago.
- The Vietnam *Memorial* is a dramatic tribute.
- Do you have a copy of yesterday's *memorandum* on the new procedures for locking up?
- My uncle has a collection of *memorabilia* from World War II.
- We *commemorate* Lincoln's birthday in February.
- Susan has *memorized* a Longfellow poem for the recital.
- Do you think the President will write his *memoirs*?

The Latin word *memor* means "mindful." The Latin word *memorandum* means "a thing to be remembered." The root that you see in the examples in the preceding sentences is *-mem-*. Some of these words—*remember, memory, memorize,* and *memorial*—are probably familiar ones. To *commemorate* is to celebrate the memory of an event; *memorabilia* are things worthy of remembrance; *memoirs* are personal rememberings or records.

-FIN-

What do the words containing the root *-fin-* in the following sentences mean?

- What is the *definition* of euphoria?
- *Finally,* I want to thank . . .
- The beach seems to have an *infinite* number of grains of sand.
- Roger is *confined* to his home while he has measles.
- Have you *finished* writing that report yet?

The Latin word *finis* means "end." *Finire* is Latin for "to finish" and "to limit." The root that you see in the examples in the preceding sentences is *-fin-*. A *definition* is the limit of something by virtue of how it is defined. To *confine* is to limit or restrict movement. *Infinite* combines the prefix *in-*, meaning "not," with *-fin-*, giving us "without end" or "without limit."

-VAR-

What do the words containing the root *-var-* in the following sentences mean?

- The *Ed Sullivan Show* was an early example of a television *variety* show.

- The route the bus takes between Maple Street and City Hall never *varies*.
- *My Fair Lady* is a *variation* on the *Pygmalion* theme.
- Nurse Bennett's caring manner is *invariable*.
- The colors in that *variegated* embroidery thread go from yellow to red.

The Latin word *varius* means "diverse" or "having differences." The root in the examples in the preceding sentences is *-var-*. *Variegated* thread, for example, varies in color, changing from one color to the next for the length of the thread. *Invariable* combines the negative prefix *in-* with the root *-var-* to give us "unchanging."

Working with Words

MULTIPLE CHOICE

Circle the letter next to the answer that best defines the italicized word. Use your knowledge of contextual clues, prefixes, and roots to help you decide.

1. How does your family *commemorate* the Fourth of July?
   - (a) cook
   - (b) celebrate
   - (c) commence
   - (d) begin

2. *Invariably,* George checks the mailbox before going into the house.
   - (a) carefully
   - (b) always
   - (c) hopefully
   - (d) variously

3. *Confine* your remarks to the subject being discussed.
   - (a) silence
   - (b) converse
   - (c) limit
   - (d) reverse

4. The cafeteria provides a *variety* of main dishes to select from.
   - (a) delicious
   - (b) ethnic
   - (c) high calorie
   - (d) several different

5. Gloria has *ascertained* that Carl was not in the office last Tuesday.
   - (a) determined
   - (b) announced
   - (c) sworn
   - (d) asserted

6. Have you read the *memoirs* of John Adams?
   - (a) personal memories
   - (b) memorandums
   - (c) armoires
   - (d) novels

7. Did the client *certify* that this is the actual letter he wrote last May?
   - (a) give assurance
   - (b) imply
   - (c) write
   - (d) infer

8. The accounting department distributed a *memorandum* about holiday pay.
   - (a) sign-up sheet
   - (b) financial report
   - (c) short notice
   - (d) time release

FILL IN THE BLANKS

From the following list, select the word that best completes each sentence and write the word in the blank space provided. Use your knowledge of roots to help you decide. Use each word only once. Use all of the words.

various	commemorate	ascertain	certain
confine	finally	finish	remember

Memorandum

TO: All Staff

FROM: Administrative Services

SUBJECT: July Holiday

DATE: June 29, 200X

We need to (1) _____ how many employees would like to leave the office early on July 3. Those of you wishing to leave the office on Thursday, July 3, after you (2) _____ your assignments for the day, may do so.

  The company is (3) _____ that many of you will (4) _____ this holiday with picnics, barbecues, and fireworks. Please (5) _____ to (6) _____ your (7) _____ activities to *safe* ones. (8) _____, return to work, relaxed and cheerful, on Monday morning.

FIND THE MISFIT

In each group, underline the word that does not belong with the others. Then state why it doesn't belong.

1. different, invariable, varied, diverse

2. variation, change, varsity, variety

3. memorize, memorial, remember, member

4. variegated, locked, distinct, varied

5. certificate, sure, certain, curtain

6. finish, end, find, final

7. confine, restrict, limit, confetti

8. commemorate, comment, celebrate, remember

USING YOUR WORDS

Use each of the following words in a sentence that demonstrates that you understand the meaning of the word.

1. infinite

2. confine

3. memorable

4. invariable

5. certify

Suffixes

Describing and Doing

SUFFIXES THAT DESCRIBE

Suffixes are word endings. Sometimes a suffix is several letters long, sometimes only one. Suffixes tell us more about a word; they help refine it or change it. Some suffixes tell us about the role of a word in a sentence: whether the word refers to a doer, a state of being, an action, or a description.

Some suffixes indicate that a word describes something. If we change *talk* to *talkative*, then a talkative person is someone who talks a lot. If we change *respond* to *responsive*, then a *responsive* politician is one who responds to our requests or opinions. Many other suffixes, like *-ive*, say "like the root." (One exception is *-less*, which indicates "lack of." *Colorless* indicates lack of color; *careless* indicates lack of caution; *guiltless* indicates innocence, or having no guilt.)

–ful, –most, –like

These three suffixes are probably the simplest and easiest to remember, because their meaning is straightforward. What do the adjectives with these suffixes mean in the following sentences?

- Max is a *cheerful* payroll clerk. (full of cheer)
- Earning high profits is *hopeful* thinking. (full of hope)
- Success is *uppermost* in her mind. (highest)
- The report is in the *rightmost* drawer. (most to the right)
- Sophia's behavior is *childlike*. (like a child)
- That ballet requires a *snakelike* motion. (like a snake)

-able, -ible

The *-able* and *-ible* endings are actually the same suffix with two spellings. The meaning is just what you might guess: "capable of." *Readable* and *legible* both mean "capable of being read." *Operable* means "capable of being operated or being operated on." *Reversible* means "capable of being reversed." If a negative prefix is part of the word, then the meaning is "not capable of." *Irreversible*, therefore, means "not capable of being reversed;" *illegible* means "not capable of being read."

The words *visible, invisible, questionable, unquestionable, convertible, variable, invariable,* and *memorable* contain roots you learned in the previous lessons. What do they mean?

-y, -ly, -ive, -ous

The suffixes *-y, -ly, -ive,* and *-ous* are among the most common word endings, though by no means the only ones, that indicate that something is being described. The suffix *-ly* indicates *how* something is done. This suffix forms adverbs, words that describe actions or states of being, rather than things. The other suffixes in this section describe people, places, or things; they form adjectives.

What do the words with these endings mean in the following sentences?

-ly
- Add these invoices *quickly*. (in a quick manner)
- She counted the change *accurately*.
- He balanced the checkbook very *carefully*.
- We were *greatly* saddened by our misfortune.

-y
- The report is too *wordy*. (having many words)
- We were very lucky to sell those old *floppy* disks.
- Don't get that *sticky* candy near the computer.
- Have the poster printed on *glossy* paper.

-ive
- She wore *corrective* shoes. (that correct)
- We need *intensive* practice.
- This group is very *supportive*.
- The computer system was *expensive*.

-ous
- He was a *famous* president. (having fame or renown; well-known)

-ious
- The coronation was a *glorious* occasion.

OTHER SUFFIXES THAT INDICATE DESCRIPTION

Many other suffixes indicate description. Among them are the following:

-ic
- *dramatic* entrance, *poetic* phrase

-ary
- *elementary* school, *honorary* title

-ed
- *satisfied* customer; *dried* ink

-al
- *final* plan, *musical* talent

-ical
- *radical* idea, a *critical* point

-an
- *urban* renewal, *Cuban* history

-ish
- *reddish* paint, *mulish* determination

-ile
- *juvenile* court, *missile* storage

SUFFIXES THAT DO

Four suffixes are commonly used to indicate action: *-ate*, *-ify*, *-ize*, and, less frequently, *-en*. Read the following passage and circle each word that ends in one of these suffixes. What does each word mean? Check yourself by reading the remainder of this lesson.

```
Memorandum

TO: All Hourly Employees

FROM: Payroll Administration

SUBJECT: New Time Cards

DATE: November 4, 200X
```

In order to simplify the reporting of employee working hours, the firm will standardize the daily time cards. Each card will identify an employee and specify a work schedule. The format of the cards will facilitate recording of hours; however, you still will calculate the total hours worked each day. We will activate the new computer program to handle the cards next week. Please utilize the new system immediately. If you have any questions, we shall be happy to listen to them.

-ate

The words ending in *-ate* in the memo are *activate*, *facilitate*, and *calculate*. Often the *-ate* suffix indicates "to make" or "to cause to be."

Activate means to "make active" or "cause to be active"; the memo refers to activating the computer program, meaning to make it active or to begin it.

The root of *facilitate* is an adjective, *facilis*, meaning "easy." The new cards will facilitate the recording of hours; they will make the recording easier.

The third *-ate* suffix is part of the word *calculate*. The root of *calculate* is a Latin word for "pebble," referring to pebbles once used for counting. To *calculate*, therefore, is to "cause to be counted." While it may be easier in this case to simply remember that *calculate* means "count" or "compute," analysis such as this will give you an advantage in figuring out meanings of many unfamiliar words, especially those with more familiar and logical roots.

How would you define *aerate* (root = "air"), *coordinate* (root = "order"), and *concentrate* (root = "center")?

-ize

Two words with the suffix *-ize* were used in the memo: *standardize* and *utilize*.

Like *-ate*, *-ize* means "to make" or "to cause to be." To *standardize* the time cards, therefore, means to make them standard, to give them a similar format. (The implication is that there had previously been various formats of cards.)

The root of *utilize* is *uti*, which means "to use." *Utilize*, therefore, means to "cause to be used" or, more simply, to "use."

How would you define *regularize*, *sympathize*, and *systematize*?

–ify

Simplify, *identify*, and *specify* appeared in the memo. As you now expect, *simplify* means "make simple" and *specify* means "make specific" or "give the details of."

Analysis of *identify* is not as straightforward. The root is *idem*, meaning "the same." We think of *identical* as meaning "the same," but you probably think of your individual *identity* as being your own and only yours. This is the sense of the root as it is used in *identify*: "one and the same, the very same, the only." Each card will cause an employee to be the one and only person for that card. (*Identify* is a case like *calculate*: Analyzing its components may be more difficult than learning its meaning from experience. The process is, nonetheless, a valuable one.)

–en

This suffix is not nearly as common as the others mentioned, but it may be more interesting. The meaning of *-en*, like the other suffixes discussed, is "to make." *Deepen* means to "make deep"; *harden*, to "make hard"; and *tighten*, to "make tight." The root *hlyst* means "hearing," so *listen* means "to make hearing." What do *strengthen* and *fasten* mean?

What makes *-en* special is that this suffix and the words it ends are derived from Old English. The roots for the preceding words are from Old English. Some descriptive words and some plurals also use the *-en* suffix and are from Old English, such as *woolen*, *waxen*, *flaxen*, *oxen*, and *children*. Experts in language and culture and history use these clues to learn about the past.

Working with Words

MULTIPLE CHOICE

Circle the letter next to the answer that best completes the sentence. Use your knowledge of contextual clues, prefixes, and roots to help you decide.

1. The project met all its goals; it was _____.
   - (a) sensible
   - (b) successful
   - (c) convertible
   - (d) goalish

2. The person in that job makes many public speeches; he or she is highly _____.
   - (a) sensible
   - (b) visible
   - (c) senseful
   - (d) indivisible

3. The firm tried to _____ all the talents of its employees.
   - (a) activize
   - (b) sensitize
   - (c) utilize
   - (d) memorize

4. We need to _____ these procedures; everyone should follow the same steps.
   - (a) sensible
   - (b) standardize
   - (c) convertible
   - (d) terminate

5. The staff will never forget that _____ day.
   - (a) memorable
   - (b) colorless
   - (c) forgetful
   - (d) priceless

6. The firm added another computer to the network in order to _____ the production of reports.
   - (a) stop
   - (b) visualize
   - (c) facilitate
   - (d) specify

7. Opening this door will _____ the alarm.
   - (a) activate
   - (b) facilitate
   - (c) calculate
   - (d) aerate

8. The bolts holding those parts together are loose; please _____ them.
   - (a) activate
   - (b) tighten
   - (c) harden
   - (d) eliminate

FILL IN THE BLANKS

From the following list, select the word that best completes each sentence and write the word in the blank space provided. Use your knowledge of context, roots, and suffixes to help you decide. Use each word only once. Use all of the words.

talkative	irreversible	invariable
hasty/hastily	saplings	illegible
priceless	simplify	joyous
carefully/careful		

1. Doctors are thought to have handwriting so poor you cannot read what they write. Their handwriting is _____.

2. Now that the procedure has begun, we cannot undo what has been done and go back. The process is _____.

3. When Mr. Kent arrives at the office, he checks for messages, reads his mail, returns important calls, and then asks for the daily sales report. This routine never changes; the order is _____.

4. Mary was in a great hurry and made her decision in haste. The decision was _____. Mary made her decision _____.

5. Sam checked the numbers in the spreadsheet with great care. He checked them _____. He was very _____.

6. The discussion continued for hours; everyone in the group had a great deal to say. The participants were _____.

7. That vase is so valuable, a price cannot be placed on it. The vase is _____.

8. The firm's president announced that the company made a profit. The occasion was a _____ one—everyone was delighted.

9. The Employees for the Environment group planted 100 _____ that would one day become large shade trees.

10. This report is very complicated; please try to make it simple. _____ it.

USING YOUR WORDS

Use each of the following words in a sentence that demonstrates that you understand the meaning of the word.

1. calculate

2. falsify

3. invariable

4. intensive

5. urban

6. priceless

Suffixes

Naming

Some suffixes work with roots to make nouns, or naming words. *Teach* is an action changed to a name by adding *-er* to give us *teacher,* "one who teaches." *Assist* is an action that is changed by adding *-ant* to give *assistant,* "one who assists." This lesson presents suffixes that form nouns or naming words.

DOERS

Many words that refer to "one who" does something end in a suffix that helps you recognize them as a person or thing that performs an action or receives an action. Find the words that refer to a "doer" or "receiver" of an action in the following announcement. Circle the words with those suffixes.

> The librarian has asked for volunteers to work next Saturday to operate the annual book sale. Any willing helper should call the library assistant before Tuesday. We particularly need a cashier for the morning. We also need a manager to help list the books that have come in from donors. Child care will be available, including a storyteller.

Did you circle *librarian, volunteers, helper, assistant, cashier, manager, donors,* and *storyteller?*

-er, -or

The suffixes *-er* and *-or* are two of the most common suffixes that indicate the doer of an action. The *-er* suffix is the more common of the two; examples include *manager* (one who manages) and *shipper* (one who ships things). How would you define an *investor*? The *-er* ending sometimes appears as *-ier*, as in *cashier* (one who takes cash payments) and *financier* (one who is skilled in finances), or *-yer*, as in *lawyer*.

Remembering which words are spelled with *-er* and which with *-or* can be quite a challenge. Some words that use the *-or* ending are *supervisor* (one who supervises), *auditor* (one who examines or adjusts accounts), *donor* (one who gives or donates), and *lessor* (one who leases something to someone else).

-ant, -ent

The suffixes *-ant* and *-ent* also refer to a person or thing that performs the action of the root. The word *assistant* in the preceding memo contains the ending *-ant*, giving us *assistant*. A *deterrent* is something that deters or hinders. A *confidant* is someone to whom secrets are confided.

Many words with ending in *-ant* and *-ent* are not "doers," but adjectives that describe a person or thing having the quality of the root, like the describing words of Lesson 18.

- The *efficient* assistant completed the job in a day. (The assistant is effective or accomplishes tasks in an effective and quick manner.)
- The effects of that change are *permanent*. (The effects will remain throughout the future.)

-an, -ian, -ist, -eer

The endings *-an, -ian, ist,* and *-eer* are less common than the other suffixes that indicate the doer of an action. The *-an/-ian* ending indicates connection with a place, person, group, doctrine, and so on. A *librarian* is one who manages a library. *Cuban, Bostonian, Californian,* and *Italian* refer to a place. *Republican* and *Libertarian* refer to doctrines.

Words with the suffix *-ist* can refer to who does the action of the root or has to do with it professionally (*sociologist, pharmacist, psychologist*) or one who supports a philosophy or idea (*socialist, idealist, capitalist*).

An *-eer* ending is usually connected to a root that is an object rather than an action and indicates one who uses or operates that object. How does this help you understand *auctioneer, puppeteer,* or *engineer*?

RECEIVERS

-ee

The suffix -ee is attached to action words to indicate the receiver of the action or the person who undergoes or is affected by an action. Compare the terms in the following examples.

> *employer, employee*   Ms. Sims, the employer, gave Mr. Roberts a pay increase. The company has six employees working in the mail room.
>
> *grantor, grantee*   The grant was given to the grantee last December. The grantor gave them a very large grant.
>
> *lessor, lessee*   Mrs. Loras, the lessor, leased her property to the city. The city, the lessee, leased the property from Mrs. Loras.

Some words ending in -ee refer to a person described by the term. An *absentee* is someone who is absent. A *devotee* is someone who is devoted, as in "a devotee of the opera."

PROCESSES AND RESULTS OF ACTIONS

Some suffixes are attached to action roots to indicate the process or the result of the action. See if you can find such words in the following memo. Circle the words with those suffixes.

```
Memorandum

TO: Product Development Team Members

FROM: Executive Staff

SUBJECT: Completion of SoftSense

DATE: August 2, 200X

We are pleased to make the announcement that the

development of our new software program, SoftSense, is

complete. We are very proud of this achievement;

everyone involved should share in our sense of
```

```
accomplishment. The solutions to the problems we met

were not always easy, but they were always found. Each

person's contribution to the effort was important; every

assignment was taken seriously. In recognition of this

milestone, a bonus will be added to each team member's

next paycheck. Congratulations to all.
```

Did you circle *announcement, development, achievement, accomplishment, solutions, contribution, assignment, recognition,* and *congratulations?*

–ment

The ending *-ment* indicates the result of an act or a process. When, for example, the suffix *-ment* is added to the action root *achieve*, we have the word *achievement,* which names the result of achieving. The verb *govern* is changed to the name of a process by adding the suffix *-ment,* giving us *government.*

In the preceding memo, the terms *announcement, development, achievement, accomplishment,* and *assignment* use the *-ment* suffix. An *announcement* is the result of announcing; a *development* is the process or result of developing; an *accomplishment* is what results from accomplishing something. The result of assigning a task to someone (or assigning an item to a category) is an *assignment.*

–ion

The ending *-tion* (and its other forms, such as *-tion, -sion, -ition,* and *-ation,*), like *-ment,* indicates the result of an act or a process. The suffix *-ation* added to the action root *compute* gives us *computation.* Likewise, when this suffix is added to *contribute,* we have the result of contributing: a *contribution.*

Some roots are changed before the suffix is added. For example, the word *conversion,* meaning the "result or process of converting something," drops the *t* from *convert* and then adds the suffix *-sion.* In the memo example, the word *solution* is the outcome of changing the action root *solv-* by dropping the *v* and then adding the suffix *-ution.*

Two other words in the memo example use the *-ion* ending: *congratulations* (the result of congratulating), and *recognition* (the result of recognizing).

QUALITY AND CONDITION

Several suffixes end words referring to the condition of something or to a quality. The most common of these are *-ance* and *-ence*. Two other important endings used with words to indicate a quality are *-cy* and *-ity*. What do the words with these endings in the following sentences mean?

- The mayor is a woman of considerable *prominence* in our *community*.
- He questioned the *importance* of this meeting.
- The ink for marking the laundry was chosen for its *permanence*.

-ance, -ence

Like *-ment* and *-ion*, the suffixes *-ance* and *-ence* can indicate a process or result of an action. For example, *performance* is the result of performing; *correspondence* is the process or the result of corresponding (for example, letters).

In some cases, these two suffixes indicate a quality or condition. *Importance* is the quality of being important; *prominence* is the quality of being prominent, standing out, or highly visible. *Permanence* refers to the condition of being permanent.

-cy, -ity

The suffixes *-cy* and *-ity* also indicate qualities. You have already learned that *scarcity* means "a lack of" and that *proximity* means "the quality of being near." *Bankruptcy* refers to being bankrupt; *secrecy* refers to being secret.

Working with Words

FILL IN THE BLANKS

From the following list, select the word that best completes each sentence and write the word in the blank space provided. Use your knowledge of context, roots, and suffixes to help you decide. Use each word only once. Use all of the words.

donor	correspondence	shipper	cashier
efficient	assistant	contribution	grantee
Bostonian	accomplishment		

1. Eloise completed the task quickly and correctly; she is _____.
2. Did you make a _____ to the Red Cross?
3. The _____ to the president helped her write the report and make the graphs for it.
4. Florence asked the _____ to label the crate clearly so that it would not get lost.
5. The _____ gave Gregory the wrong change.
6. Which _____ gave the most blood this month?
7. Our team built the smallest tower, but we were proud of our _____.
8. Who writes the responses to _____ from disssatisfied customers?
9. Can you tell he is _____ from his Massachusetts accent?
10. Do you know when the _____ will receive the money from the grantor?

WORD COMPLETION

Complete each word in the left-hand column by adding one of the following suffixes. Then match the completed word with its definition in the right-hand column. Write the letter of the correct definition next to the completed word.

-eer	-or	-ant	-ent
-ian	-ee	-er	-ment

1. librar _____   a. one who leases something from someone

2. auction _____   b. one who leases something to someone

3. less _____   c. one who is responsible for a library

4. perman _____   d. one who teaches

5. less _____   e. one who helps

6. assist _____   f. something completed

7. accomplish _____   g. not temporary

8. teach _____   h. one who conducts an auction

USING YOUR WORDS

Use each of the following words in a sentence that demonstrates that you understand the meaning of the word.

1. supervisor

2. efficient

3. pharmacist

4. employee

5. accomplishment

6. correspondence

Section 3 Review

The lessons in Section 3 presented some common prefixes, roots, and suffixes. Review the following prefixes, roots, and suffixes and their meanings. Examples of words containing these parts are given in parentheses. (While many of these word parts may have more than one meaning, the most common usage is listed.)

PREFIXES

Size and Amount

micro- small (microscope)

mini- small (minivan)

macro- large (macro command)

magn- large (magnify)

maxi- large (maximum)

mega- large (megabyte)

Negation

non- not (nonsmoking)

un- not (unlikely); with verbs, *un-* indicates a reversal (unlock)

in-, im-, il- not (insufficient, immobile, illogical)

dis- not (dishonest); with verbs, *dis-* can indicate reversal (disjoin)

a- not (atypical); in, on, at (asleep); up, on (arise); of (akin)

All, Many, Partial, Half

multi- many (multicolored)

poly- many (polytechnic)

omni- all (omnivorous)

pan- all (panorama)

semi- partial (semiorganized)

hemi- half (hemisphere)

over- too much (overbaked)

hyper- too much (hyperactive)

extra- additional or extreme (extravagant)

ultra- extremely (ultramodern)

super- extra (superfluous)

hypo- too little or lacking (hypothesis)

under- lacking (underweight)

Number

mono- one (monocle)

uni- one (unify)

bi- two (bicycle)

di- two (dioxide)

diplo- two (diplomat)

du- two (duet)

tri- three (trifold)

deca- ten (decade)

cent- hundred (centigrade)

milli- thousandth (milligram)

kilo- thousand (kilogram)

Before or After

post- after (postscript)

after- after (afterthought)

fore- before (foreground)

pre- before (preschool)

pro- before (prologue); through (proceed)

ante- before (antedate)

Place

ex- out (export)

im- in (import)

intro- in (introvert)

extra- out (extraordinary)

inter- among (interdisciplinary)

per- through (permanent)

trans- across (trans-Atlantic)

circum- around (circumscribe)

peri- around (periscope)

re- back (recline)

retro- back (retrospect)

com-, con-, co- with, together (committee, connect, cooperate)

syn-, syl-, sym- with, together (synthesis, syllable, sympathetic)

Good or Bad

bene- good, well (benefit)

mal- bad, ill (malevolent)

mis- bad, wrong (mistake)

ROOTS

-scop- look at, see (microscope)

-spect-, -spectr- look at, see (spectator, spectrum)

-vid-, -vis- see (evidence, vision)

-dict- tell, say (dictate)

-scrib-, -script- write (scribble, prescription)

-leg-, -lect- read (legible, lecture)

-quer-, -quire-, -quest- ask (query, inquire, question)

-port- carry (portable)

-fer- carry (transfer)

-mit-, -mis- sent (transmit, submission)

-vert-, -vers- turn (revert, reverse)

-cert- determine (certify)

-fin- end (finish)

-mem- mindful (remember)

-var- diverse (various)

SUFFIXES

-ful full of (wonderful)

-most most (topmost)

-like like, similar to (childlike)

-able, -ible able (memorable, legible)

-y indicates description (airy)

-ly indicates description (gladly)

-ive indicates description (descriptive)

-ous indicates description (famous)

-ic indicates description (dramatic)

-ed indicates description (satisfied)

-al indicates description (final)

-ical indicates description (musical)

-an indicates description (urban)

-ish indicates description (owlish)

-ile indicates description (juvenile)

-ate to make or cause to be (calculate)

-ize to make or cause to be (utilize)

-ify to make or cause to be (justify)

-en to make or cause to be (strengthen)

Doers

-er one who or thing that (teacher, eraser)

-or one who or thing that (donor, elevator)

-ant one who or thing that (assistant, deodorant)

-cy quality or condition (bankruptcy)

-ity quality or condition (scarcity)

-ent one who or thing that (dissident, deterrent)

-an, -ian related to a place, person, group, and so on (Californian)

-eer one who (auctioneer)

-ee indicates recipient of an action (grantee)

-ment indicates result or process (achievement, government)

-ion, -tion, -sion, etc. indicates result or process (transition)

-ance result or process (performance); quality (importance)

-ence result or process (correspondence); quality (permanence)

Working with Words

FILL IN THE BLANKS

From the list on pages 144–146, select the prefix that best completes the italicized word and write the prefix in the blank space provided. Use your knowledge of context, roots, and prefixes to help you decide. Use each prefix spelling only once. You will not use all of the prefixes.

1. The _____ *mum* passing score is 60; the _____ *mum* possible is 80.

2. The information was _____ *sufficient* for us to make a decision, so we requested more data.

3. The biologist examined the organisms under a _____ *scope*.

4. Because Greta has moved to Seattle, it is _____ *likely* that she will come to New York for the party.

5. Parking on this street during the week is _____ *legal;* if you do not move your car you will get a ticket.

6. Some of the exercises included _____ *ple*-choice questions.

7. After working all day to bring some order to his work station, Harvey's desk was still only _____ *organized.*

8. Iris eats more than any of us, but she is still _____ *weight.*

9. The staff usually disagrees about the smoking policy, but this time they presented a _____ *fied* argument.

10. This business arranges for manufacturers to _____ *port* materials into the country and then to _____ *port* finished products to foreign buyers. (*Hint:* Use two different prefixes.)

11. This fertilizer will be most _____ *ficial* to the nursery's plants.

12. When will the executive _____ *mittee* discuss the marketing plan?

13. How will the firm _____ *port* the goods from the warehouse to its local stores?

14. Will the change be _____ *manent* or temporary?

FILL IN THE BLANKS

From the list on pages 146–147, select the suffix that best completes the italicized word and write the suffix in the blank space provided. Use your knowledge of context, roots, and suffixes to help you decide. Use each suffix spelling only once. You will not use all of the suffixes.

1. We should *personal* _____ these form letters so that the readers feel that we are writing to them as individuals.

2. This report is very complex; please *simpl* _____ it.

3. Add more facts and figures to this report in order to *strength* _____ our arguments.

4. These order forms should be *standard* _____ so that their format is similar and all the necessary questions are asked every time the form is used.

5. Entering the information in the computer will *facilit* _____ the preparation of the report.

6. Jane's handwriting is *illeg* _____ so she dictates all of her memos and letters.

7. The graduating class never forgot the dean's *memor* _____ speech.

8. Leo is *hope* _____ that he will receive an increase in pay.

9. The managers were unhappy because the products were being finished too *slow* _____.

10. The Myers Company is the largest *employ* _____ in our town; more than 20,000 *employ* _____ currently work there.

11. Nell hired a new administrative *assist* _____ to help with preparing the budgets.

12. We were very pleased with our *accomplish* _____.

13. Olivia evaluated Parker's *perform* _____ in the new job.

14. Finally we found a *solut* _____ to the problem.

FILL IN THE BLANKS

From the following list, select the word that best completes each sentence and write the word in the blank space provided. Use the sentence context and your knowledge of prefixes, roots, and suffixes to help you decide. Use each word only once. Use all of the words. (*Hint:* Read the list of words *before* reading the sentences.)

subscription	certify	revision	variety	transportation
utilize	conversion	defer	perspective	proceed

1. The printer provided a _____ of types of paper for us to choose from.

2. The accounting department must _____ that the figures in the annual report are accurate.

3. The _____ of goods from the manufacturer to the marketplace is very costly.

4. Which overnight delivery service do we _____ to send our urgent packages?

5. When will the _____ to the new computer system be complete? This change has been taking a long time.

6. The presentations will _____ immediately after intermission.

7. Have we ordered a _____ to *The Wall Street Journal* or *The New York Times?*

8. Roger was informed that Quall Ink Company would _____ payment for one month and would pay the entire amount due at that time.

9. This document is the third _____ of the company's report to the board of directors.

10. Stella asked for Tim's _____ on the question of expanding the sales division this year.

USING YOUR WORDS (REVIEW)

Use each of the following words or phrases in a sentence that demonstrates that you understand the meaning of the word or phrase.

1. permission to transfer

2. contradictory statements

3. spectators' description

4. illegible notes

5. international agreement

6. pan-American highway

7. donors' contributions

8. portable

9. multicolored

10. certificate

11. invariable steps

12. computation

Section 4
Troublemakers

Some words in our language persistently cause problems. Words that share the same spelling or sound similar, or both, can be easily confused. Mistakes in using these words can be embarrassing because their meanings are different, and in business situations you are expected to use them correctly. These lessons on "troublemakers" will teach you to recognize and use these terms correctly.

The following pairs are the troublemakers covered in Lessons 21 through 24:

accept, except	discreet, discrete
access, excess	disinterested, uninterested
affect, effect	elicit, illicit
allusion, illusion	eminent, imminent
anecdote, antidote	perquisite, prerequisite
capital, capitol	precede, proceed
council, counsel	principal, principle
disburse, disperse	stationary, stationery

WHAT DO YOU KNOW?

Circle the word in parentheses that best completes each sentence.

1. Stella completed all of the pages (accept / except) page 31.

2. What (affect / effect) will the budget cuts have on the local schools?

3. Great! That's a (capital / capitol) idea!

4. The (council / counsel) will meet next Tuesday.

5. Who will (disburse / disperse) the funds when the accounts become available?

6. The disputing family members requested a (disinterested / uninterested) person to make a decision.

7. The physician was an (eminent / imminent) professional in the medical world.

8. The radio announced that the arrival of the hurricane along the coast was (eminent / imminent).

9. He refused to agree to the terms of the settlement not because of money but as a matter of (principal / principle).

10. Use the (stationary / stationery) that has just arrived from the printer.

HOW DID YOU DO?

(1) except; (2) effect; (3) capital; (4) council; (5) disburse; (6) disinterested; (7) eminent; (8) imminent; (9) principle; (10) stationery

Troublemakers 1

ACCEPT, EXCEPT

Although these two terms sound very much alike and, indeed, have the same root, they are very different in meaning: One combines the root meaning "to take" with the prefix meaning "in"; the other combines the root with the prefix meaning "out." Read the following examples and then answer the preview questions.

- The committee asked Jennifer to *accept* the award for creativity.
- Management *accepted* the report as accurate.
- Everyone was present *except* Henry.
- Send Dan all of the files *except* the customer file.

1. Which term means "to take in" or "to receive"? _____

2. Which means "leaving out," "aside from," or "excluding"? _____

When you *accept* something, you receive it. Sometimes *accepting* something indicates approval of it, as in the second example. *Except* means that something is being left out. Remember that the prefix *ex-* means "out" and you will use *except* correctly every time.

ACCESS, EXCESS

This pair of terms has the same sound-similarity problem as *accept* and *except*. Read the following examples and then answer the preview questions.

- Boyce has *access* to the computer.
- Carmen is the only person with *access* to the warehouse at night.
- Is there any *excess* money in the budget?
- What did Dave do with the *excess* food?

1. Which term means "coming near" or "permission to enter"?

   _____

2. Which means "more than needed" or "surplus"? _____

When you have *access* to something, it is available to you. *Excess* means "extra" or "more than is needed."

AFFECT, EFFECT

One of these words means to "influence." The same word can also mean "feeling" or "emotion." The other refers to bringing about a result or to the result itself. Read the following examples and then answer the preview questions.

- How did the decision *affect* employee attitudes?
- Will the budget cuts *affect* salaries?
- With jaw tense and fist clenched, he spoke with great *affect*.
- What was the *effect* of the new system on productivity?
- How can we *effect* the change most quickly?

1. What are the two meanings or uses of the word *affect*?

   _____

2. What are the two meanings or uses of the word *effect*?

   _____

The word *affect*, as used in the first two examples, means "influence." As this word is used in the third example, *affect* means "feeling."

The fourth sentence uses *effect* in the meaning of "result." In the last sentence, *effect* is used to mean "bring about" or "make happen."

ALLUSION, ILLUSION

The written difference between these two terms is quite clear: They begin with different letters. However, the difference between the two terms in sound is very slight. *Allusion* is pronounced beginning with a sound similar to the *a* in *about*; *illusion* begins with a sound like *i* in *ill*. Read the following examples and then answer the preview questions.

- The manager made an *allusion* to a possible wage increase during the conversation.
- Is there an *allusion* to death in that poem?
- The fancy building gives the *illusion* that the firm is wealthy.
- Playing sports gives grandfather an *illusion* of youth.

1. Which word means "an indirect reference"? _____

2. Which means "a false idea"? _____

An *allusion* is an indirect reference or hint. An *illusion* is a false idea.

Working with Words

MULTIPLE CHOICE

Circle the letter next to the answer that best completes the sentence. Use your knowledge of context clues, prefixes, and roots to help you decide.

1. While the speaker appeared to be very cool, his voice during the speech was filled with _____.
   - (a) allusion
   - (b) affect
   - (c) illusion
   - (d) effect

2. Houdini, the famous magician, was a master of _____.
   - (a) profusion
   - (b) derision
   - (c) allusion
   - (d) illusion

3. Will the new computer _____ your work?
   - (a) excess
   - (b) affect
   - (c) affirm
   - (d) except

4. Who has _____ to the building on weekends?
   - (a) access
   - (b) allusion
   - (c) excess
   - (d) illusion

5. Please _____ our apologies for the error on your invoice.
   - (a) affect
   - (b) access
   - (c) accept
   - (d) except

6. We need to _____ changes in the firm's work schedules.
   - (a) effect
   - (b) excess
   - (c) except
   - (d) affirm

7. _____ for Tuesday, we add the cash at four; Tuesdays we do it at six.
   - (a) Extra
   - (b) Excess
   - (c) Accept
   - (d) Except

8. What _____ did the new building heater have on energy use?
   - (a) accept
   - (b) effect
   - (c) time
   - (d) allusion

FIND THE MISFIT

In each group, underline the word that does not belong with the others. Then state why it doesn't belong.

1. illusion, appraisal, unreal, magic

2. outcome, affect, effect, result

3. leave out, except, all but, excess

4. reference, alluring, allusion, hint

5. excess, extra, except, additional

6. availability, access, path, computer

7. accept, take, except, receive

8. emotion, effect, affect, feeling

FILL IN THE BLANKS

From the following list, select the word that best completes each sentence and write the word in the blank space provided. Use your knowledge of "troublemakers" and sentence context to help you decide. Use each word only once. Use all of the words.

illusion	allusion	accept	effect
excess	access	except	affect

1. I need _____ to the supply room in order to take inventory tonight.
2. The disappearance was just an _____.
3. She refused to _____ the statements in the report as accurate.

4. What _____ did the new environmental protection regulations have on the factory's waste disposal?

5. The article made an _____ to possible fraud on the part of the chief accounting officer.

6. The plan is complete _____ for estimating final costs.

7. Can we rent out the _____ storage space?

8. Although Frank's magazine article was supposed to be highly objective, it was written with great _____.

USING YOUR WORDS

Use each of the following words in a sentence that demonstrates that you understand the meaning of the word.

1. accept

2. except

3. illusion

4. excess

5. effect

6. affect

7. access

8. allusion

Troublemakers 2

This lesson presents four more "troublemaker" pairs. Read the examples provided in the lesson carefully, making sure you are aware of the different uses of the terms. Notice any differences in spelling. In some cases, the differences appear only in the written words, not in the pronunciation.

ANECDOTE, ANTIDOTE

One of these words means a short, entertaining story. The other is something that counteracts the effects of poison; a prefix meaning "against" should help tell you this one. Read the following examples and then answer the preview questions.

- My grandfather tells us amusing *anecdotes* about his boyhood.
- Glenda told us an *anecdote* about her last shopping spree.
- What is the *antidote* for the poison cyanide?
- An *antidote* for snakebite poison is in the first-aid kit.

1. Which word means "short story"? _____

2. Which word means "something that fights poison"?

_____

The prefix *anti-* means "against." An *antidote* works against the effects of poison. An *anecdote* is a brief, interesting story.

CAPITAL, CAPITOL

The building in which a state legislature convenes is called one of these. The other word has several meanings, including a city or town that is the seat of government of a state or nation, a type of letter, money or wealth, and first quality. Read the following examples and then answer the preview questions.

- *Capital* idea, Henry! We shall begin at once!
- Do we have enough *capital* to start a small business?
- The *capital* of California is Sacramento.
- They are voting on that issue in the *capitol* today.

1. Which word refers to a building? _____

2. Which word refers to a city? _____

Capitol refers to the statehouse or building where the state legislature convenes. (Think of the *o* as standing for *office*.) When this word is capitalized, it stands for the office building of the U.S. Congress: the *Capitol*.

The word *capital* represents the other meanings and uses mentioned above. This word also is used to refer to the death penalty: *capital* punishment.

COUNCIL, COUNSEL

These terms are not uncommon and are, therefore, important ones to use correctly. One means to "advise"; the other refers to a committee. Read the following examples and then answer the preview questions.

- The *council* will meet at two this afternoon.
- The question will be considered at the *council* meeting.
- The firm asked their lawyers to *counsel* them in the matter of bankruptcy.
- Please *counsel* us concerning the two rules.

1. Which word means "advise"? _____

2. Which word means "committee"? _____

A *council* is a committee. To *counsel* is to "give advice." *Counsel* can also be used as a noun, meaning the advice itself. A third use of *counsel* is to mean lawyer, as in "Counsel advised her to remain silent." (*Hint*: Think of the second *c* in *council* as standing for *committee*.)

DISBURSE, DISPERSE

Both of these words begin with the prefix *dis-*, which means "away." One of the words combines the prefix with the root *bourse*, meaning "purse," to give us the meaning "out of the purse" or "to pay out." The other word combines the prefix with a root that means "to scatter." We use the term to mean just that: to scatter. Read the following examples and then answer the preview questions.

- The firm will *disburse* the profits to its shareholders.
- When will the money from the sale of the house be *disbursed?*
- The cats *dispersed* when they heard the dog bark.
- The sun came out and *dispersed* the clouds.

1. Which word means "pay out" or "expend"? _____

2. Which word means "scatter"? _____

Disburse is the word meaning "pay out" or "expend." *Disperse* means "scatter." (*Hint:* Imagine taking coins out of the top of the open *u* in *disburse.*)

Working with Words

MULTIPLE CHOICE

Circle the letter next to the answer that best completes the sentence. Use the sentence context to help you decide.

1. Present your side of the issue in person to the _____ members.
   (a) counsel
   (b) correspondent
   (c) council
   (d) consolation

2. The movers are putting new furniture in the _____.
   (a) counsel
   (b) capital
   (c) capitol
   (d) caption

3. Quick! Get an _____ for the poison he swallowed!
   (a) axiom
   (b) antimony
   (c) anecdote
   (d) antidote

4. When will the bank _____ the funds we inherited?
   (a) disburse
   (b) distend
   (c) disperse
   (d) dispel

5. Harold was telling us an interesting _____ when the doorbell interrupted him. We never heard the end of the story.
   (a) axiom
   (b) antimony
   (c) anecdote
   (d) antidote

6. Where did Irene obtain the _____ to finance her flower shop?
   (a) Capital
   (b) capital
   (c) capitol
   (d) Capitol

7. Jake asked his brother to _____ him about handling the situation.
   (a) counsel
   (b) console
   (c) council
   (d) court

8. The children playing in the alley _____ when they saw the police car come around the corner.
   (a) disbursed
   (b) dispelled
   (c) dispersed
   (d) displayed

FIND THE MISFIT

In each group, underline the word that does not belong with the others. Then state why it doesn't belong.

1. committee, counsel, group, council

2. disband, disperse, scatter, disburse

3. office, capitol, Capitol, capital

4. advise, count, recommend, counsel

5. tale, story, antidote, anecdote

6. expend, pay out, disperse, disburse

7. capital, capitol, building, statehouse

8. counsel, consolation, guidance, opinion

FILL IN THE BLANKS

From the following list, select the word that best completes each sentence and write the word in the blank space provided. Use your knowledge of "troublemakers" and sentence context to help you decide. Use each word only once. Use all of the words.

anecdote	capital	capitol	council
counsel	antidote	disperse	disburse

1. Is there an _____ for arsenic?
2. Unfortunately, there were no funds to _____.
3. What is the address of the _____?

4. Kelly entertained us with her _____ about the trip to Ireland.

5. What would you _____ the firm to do under these circumstances?

6. The town _____ will vote on that issue next week.

7. The _____ is in the center of the state.

8. Loretta _____ d all the marbles to the far corners of the room with a single shot.

USING YOUR WORDS

Use each of the following words in a sentence that demonstrates that you understand the meaning of the word.

1. anecdote

2. capitol

3. capital

4. disburse

5. counsel

6. council

7. antidote

8. disperse

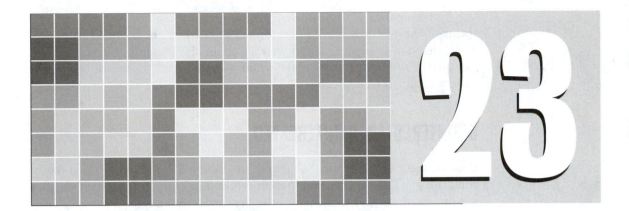

Troublemakers 3

Some troublemakers differ from one another because they have the same root but different prefixes. Your familiarity with the meanings of roots and prefixes will often help you decide which meaning is appropriate.

Other troublemakers developed from the same root and prefix but now have different spellings and meanings. The first word pair below is such a case: *Discreet* and *discrete* are derived from the same root and prefix.

DISCREET, DISCRETE

One of these terms indicates that something is not connected to anything else. The other indicates that tact and good judgment are being used; this term often refers to judgment regarding dealing with other people. Read the following examples and then answer the preview questions.

- That division of the company is a *discrete* unit; it has its own personnel, operations, and sales departments.
- When you talk with Malcolm, be *discreet* about the sale of the firm—we don't want the news to get to the competition.

1. If something is a separate unit, not connected to anything else, it is said to be _____.

2. When a person uses tact and good judgment when dealing with others, that person is said to be _____.

To be separate is to be *discrete*; to use tact is to be *discreet*. While these forms of the two words are very similar, when they are changed to nouns, the difference is greater. When we talk about the condition of being separate, we talk about its *discreteness*; when we talk about the use of tact, however, we talk about *discretion*.

DISINTERESTED, UNINTERESTED

One of these terms means "objective or unbiased" or "having no stake in something." The other means "not interested in" something. Read the following examples and then answer the preview questions.

- The two landowners presented their cases to a *disinterested* judge.
- Norton was *uninterested* and fell asleep.

1. A referee is supposed to be _____.

2. If you are bored by something, you are _____.

To have no stake in something is to be *disinterested*; to find something not very interesting is to be *uninterested*.

ELICIT, ILLICIT

These terms are among those most frequently used incorrectly. Pay close attention to the prefixes. One word means "draw out"; the other means "illegal." Read the following examples and then answer the preview questions.

- The survey was designed to *elicit* information about buying habits.
- Try to *elicit* a positive response to your request.
- Bribery is an *illicit* act.
- An *illicit* behavior that bankers worry about is check forgery.

1. Which of these words means "unlawful"? _____

2. If you draw out a response from someone, you _____ it.

Illicit means "unlawful"; *elicit* means "draw out" or "bring out." The prefixes will help you remember which is which: *Illicit* begins with the same *il-* ("not") prefix as *illegal*, both meaning "unlawful"; *elicit* begins with the prefix *e-*, a form of *ex-*, for "away" or "out."

EMINENT, IMMINENT

One of these terms means "high in station" or "famous," while the other refers to something that is about to happen. Read the following examples and then answer the preview questions.

- The award was given to an *eminent* physician.
- The *eminent* professor was elected to the school board.
- The author had waited for months; finally publication of his novel was *imminent*.
- Change was *imminent*; everyone was prepared.

1. That attorney works for the most _____ law firm in the city.

2. We heard on the radio that the arrival of the storm is _____.

Eminent means "famous" or "lofty." Someone or something that is *eminent* "stands out." *Imminent* indicates something that is about to happen and often refers to something dangerous.

Working with Words

MULTIPLE CHOICE

Circle the letter next to the answer that best completes each sentence. Use your knowledge of context clues, prefixes, and roots to help you decide.

1. The program consists of six _____ parts.
   (a) silent   (c) eminent
   (b) discrete   (d) discreet

2. Oliver, a psychology major, was _____ in the book about horses.
   (a) unintentional   (c) uninterested
   (b) discrete   (d) illicit

3. In order to _____ more responses to the ad, the firm offered a ten percent discount.
   (a) emanate   (c) eliminate
   (b) elicit   (d) illicit

4. The council discovered that the _____ politician had been covering up some illegal uses of campaign funds.
   (a) eminent   (c) elicit
   (b) discrete   (d) imminent

5. At the moment in the drama when the arrival of the evil spirits was _____, the curtain fell for intermission.
   (a) discrete   (c) uninterested
   (b) eminent   (d) imminent

6. The lecture was long and the students were not very _____ about hiding their boredom; some yawned and fell asleep.
   (a) discreet   (c) discovered
   (b) distinct   (d) discrete

7. Find a _____ person to help you settle your dispute.
   (a) disputable   (c) disinterested
   (b) disoriented   (d) diluted

8. Following the _____ transfer of funds, the clerk was dismissed from the job.
   (a) illicit   (c) diluted
   (b) illusory   (d) uninterested

FIND THE MATCH

Circle the word or phrase that is closest in meaning to each italicized word.

1. *elicit:* eliminate, draw out, illicit
2. *eminent:* emanate, prominent, emigrant
3. *discreet:* disoriented, diplomatic, distinct, destructive
4. *disinterested:* fair, bored, poor, safe
5. *illicit:* unreadable, careless, unlawful, unlicensed
6. *imminent:* about to leave, about to happen, about to mine, not small
7. *discrete:* boring, singular, undone, soft, separate
8. *uninterested:* fair, singular, bored, paid

FILL IN THE BLANKS

From the following list, select the word that best completes each sentence and write the word in the blank space provided. Use your knowledge of "troublemakers" and sentence context to help you decide. Use each word only once. Use all of the words.

discreet	disinterested	discrete	illicit
uninterested	elicit	eminent	imminent

1. Rob, _____ in the topic of today's lecture, was writing a letter to a friend rather than taking notes.

2. The _____ physician was nominated for an international award in science.

3. The survey was designed to _____ information about spending habits among young homeowners.

4. The new division is not connected to ours; it is a _____ unit.

5. The decision, a fair one, was made by a _____ judge.

6. Another term for illegal or unlawful is _____.

7. Employees in the payroll department should be _____ about other employees' salaries.

8. When the radio broadcast that the storm was _____, the townspeople hurried for shelter.

USING YOUR WORDS

Use each of the following words in a sentence that demonstrates that you understand the meaning of the word.

1. disinterested

2. discrete

3. elicit

4. eminent

5. imminent

Troublemakers 4

When you find troublemakers in your reading, both the context and the spelling help you know which meaning is intended. When you hear one of the terms in a conversation, discussion, or comment, however, you have only the context to indicate the meaning. Remember to use the context clues you learned in Section 1 to help you determine the meanings of troublemakers.

PERQUISITE, PREREQUISITE

Examining the root and prefix carefully will tell you which of these terms means "required before." The other term means "a payment or benefit that is made in addition to regular wages." Read the following examples and then answer the preview questions.

- An elementary class is often *prerequisite* to an intermediate class.
- Have you completed the *prerequisites* for this course?
- One of the *perquisites* of that job is a car allowance.
- As a *perquisite* of his job, Vic is allowed use of the company jet.

1. Which term means "required before"? _____

2. Which term is a payment? _____

A *prerequisite* is something that is required before something else can happen. A *perquisite* (or "perq") is an extra benefit or payment.

PRECEDE, PROCEED

Pay very close attention to the prefixes of these terms. One term means "go before" and the other means "go forward." Read the following examples and then answer the preview questions.

- When listed in alphabetical order, Tonia *precedes* Ursula.
- The ten o'clock news *precedes* the late-night movie.
- Please *proceed* with your presentation immediately after the break.
- Will the firm *proceed* to produce the new item after the strike?

1. Which term means "go before"? _____

2. Which term means "go forward"? _____

The prefix *pre-*, meaning "before," combines with the root *-ced-*, meaning "to go," to give us *precede*, or "go before." The prefix *per-*, meaning "through," combines with the same root to give us "go ahead" or "go forward." Note that in this case the root is spelled differently, even though it has the same meaning, "to go."

PRINCIPAL, PRINCIPLE

The root of these words, *princ-*, means "first" or "basic." One of these words refers to a rule or law. The other means someone or something that is first in rank; this term can also mean an amount of money that is owed or that is earning interest. Read the following examples and then answer the preview questions.

- That theory is based on *principles* of physics.
- He is said to be a man of very high *principles*.
- How much is the *principal* of your loan?
- The *principal* reason that Wallace changed jobs was the opportunity for advancement in the new company.

1. Which term refers to a rule? _____

2. Which term refers to someone who is first in rank, such as the head of a school? _____

A *principle* is a rule or law. *Principal* means "main," "chief," or "first in importance." *Principal* also refers to an amount of money.

STATIONARY, STATIONERY

The only difference in the spelling of these two words is the *-ary* and *-ery* endings. One of these terms refers to something that cannot be moved, something that is fixed in its location. The other means "paper for writing letters."

- The new company *stationery* has the company motto at the top.
- Did you order enough *stationery* to answer all the customer letters?
- The copying machine is on wheels; it is not *stationary*.
- Attach the tub to the wall with bolts so that it is *stationary*.

1. Which term means "paper for writing"? _____

2. Which means "unmovable"? _____

Stationary is the term that indicates that something is fixed in one location. *Stationery* refers to letter-writing paper. (*Hint:* Think of the *e* in *stationery* as standing for *envelopes*.)

Working with Words

MULTIPLE CHOICE

Circle the letter next to the answer that best completes the sentence. Use your knowledge of context clues, prefixes, and roots to help you decide.

1. Two years of experience is a _____ for taking that seminar.
   - (a) percolate
   - (b) perquisite
   - (c) prerequisite
   - (d) precedence

2. Use gray paper for printing the _____.
   - (a) stationary
   - (b) stationery
   - (c) pens
   - (d) computers

3. The meetings will _____ as planned.
   - (a) proceed
   - (b) preview
   - (c) precede
   - (d) process

4. The _____ concern of our accountant is accuracy.
   - (a) principle
   - (b) preliminary
   - (c) preventive
   - (d) principal

5. Is that machine _____, or can it be moved easily?
   - (a) stationary
   - (b) inoperative
   - (c) stationery
   - (d) expensive

6. Wanda's introduction will _____ Mel's reading of the minutes.
   - (a) eliminate
   - (b) precut
   - (c) precede
   - (d) prerequisite

7. What are the basic _____ of geometry that apply to measuring that field?
   - (a) angles
   - (b) principals
   - (c) principles
   - (d) preliminaries

8. Does the computer course have any _____ that must be fulfilled beforehand?
   - (a) perquisites
   - (b) prerequisites
   - (c) principles
   - (d) principals

FIND THE MATCH

Circle the word or phrase that is closest in meaning to each italicized word.

1. *perquisite:* benefit, percolate, accidental
2. *prerequisite:* confused, ordered, required
3. *precede:* be ahead, be behind, be finished
4. *proceed:* continue, process, preliminary
5. *principal:* friend, main, financial
6. *principle:* main, rule, prince
7. *stationary:* flying, permanent, letters
8. *stationery:* fixed, paper, railroad

FILL IN THE BLANKS

From the following list, select the word that best completes each sentence and write the word in the blank space provided. Use your knowledge of "troublemakers" and sentence context to help you decide. Use each word only once. Use all of the words.

stationary	precede	perquisite	principal
prerequisite	principle	stationery	proceed

1. Our mainframe computer is _____, but all our sales representatives have laptop computers.
2. We shall _____ with the meeting after the fire drill.
3. Which speaker is scheduled to _____ Mr. Scott, and which will follow him?
4. Is free use of the library a _____ of this job?
5. Did the new _____ arrive in time to be used for the invitations?
6. What is the _____ of gravitational pull on the tides?
7. The _____ asked the teachers to evaluate the new textbooks.
8. Is Math 101 a _____ to Computer Basics?

USING YOUR WORDS

Use each of the following words in a sentence that demonstrates that you understand the meaning of the word.

1. precede

2. proceed

3. prerequisite

4. principle

5. principal

6. stationery

Section 4 Review

The lessons in Section 4 presented words that are commonly confused. Review the following list of troublemakers and their meanings. Test yourself by covering the terms, reading the definitions, and then recalling the term. Practice with a friend by listening to the definition and supplying the word. Then listen to the term and state the definition. Think of sentences using the terms correctly.

accept   to receive

access   availability

affect   to influence

allusion   indirect reference; hint

anecdote   brief, interesting story

antidote   something that works against the effects of poison

capital   city or town that is the seat of government; type of letter; money; first quality

capitol   building where state legislature meets

council   committee

counsel   advice; to advise; lawyer

disburse   to pay out

discreet   using tact and good judgment, especially regarding other people

discrete   separate

disinterested   objective; having no stake in something

disperse   to scatter

effect   result; to make happen

elicit   draw out, bring out

eminent   prominent, famous

except   excluding

excess   extra, surplus

illicit   unlawful

illusion   false idea

imminent   about to happen

perquisite   extra benefit or payment

precede   to go before

prerequisite   something required before something else can happen

principal   main, primary; leader

principle   rule

proceed   to go forward

stationary   fixed, immobile

stationery   paper for letters

uninterested   not interested

Working with Words

WORD SELECTION

Circle the word in parentheses that best completes each sentence.

1. What (affect / effect) did the weather have on the football game?
2. Houdini, the famous magician, was a master of (allusion / illusion).
3. The movers are putting new furniture in the (capital / capitol).
4. When will the bank (disburse / disperse) the funds we inherited?
5. Where did Irene obtain the (capitol / capital) to finance her flower shop?
6. Jake asked Cora to (counsel / council) him about handling the situation.
7. The children playing in the alley (disbursed / dispersed) when they saw the police car come around the corner.
8. Who has (access / excess) to the warehouse at night?
9. Please (accept / except) our check for ten dollars.
10. Demonstration of math ability is a (prerequisite / perquisite) for taking that seminar.
11. The concert will (proceed / precede) with a new conductor.
12. Can that table be moved easily, or is it (stationary / stationery)?
13. Wanda's introduction will (precede / proceed) Mel's reading of the minutes.
14. This financial report has been prepared according to standard accounting (principles / principals).
15. In order to (elicit / illicit) more voluntary donations, they advertised the campaign.
16. Find a (disinterested / disoriented) person to help you settle your dispute.

FIND THE MISFIT

In each group, underline the word that does not belong with the others. Then state why it doesn't belong.

1. unreadable, illicit, unlawful, illegal

2. tale, story, antidote, anecdote

3. expend, pay out, disperse, disburse

4. primary, main, friend, principal

5. advise, council, recommend, counsel

6. proceed, continue, process, go forward

7. objective, bored, disinterested, fair

8. rule, prince, law, principle

9. about to occur, imminent, eminent, about to happen

10. counsel, consolation, guidance, opinion

11. uninterested, bored, not interested, without money

12. movable, stationery, letter paper, writing paper

13. discrete, boring, separate, stand-alone

14. capital, capitol, building, statehouse

15. not movable, movable, stationary, fixed in place

16. office, capitol, Capitol, capital

17. predate, precede, go forward, go before

18. reference, alluring, allusion, hint

19. outcome, affect, effect, result

20. emotion, effect, affect, feeling

21. excess, extra, except, surplus

22. accept, take, except, receive

23. illusion, illustration, unreal, magic

24. exclude, except, all but, excess

25. extra payment, percolate, perquisite, benefit

26. disband, disperse, scatter, disburse

27. disoriented, diplomatic, discreet, tactful

28. prerequisite, necessary, unnecessary, required

29. emanate, eminent, prominent, outstanding

30. elicit, bring out, draw out, illicit

31. committee, counsel, group, council

32. availability, access, path, computer

USING YOUR WORDS (REVIEW)

For each of the following words, write *either* a sentence using the word correctly *or* a brief explanation of its use.

1. access

2. anecdote

3. capitol

4. counsel

5. disburse

6. discrete

7. disinterested

8. effect

9. eminent

10. except

11. illicit

12. illusion

13. principal

14. proceed

15. stationery

16. prerequisite

Use each of the following phrases in a sentence that demonstrates that you understand the meaning of the phrase.

1. the eminent professor

2. will proceed

3. standard principles of accounting

4. is stationary

5. important perquisite

6. except yellow

7. excess space

8. positive effect

9. allusion to

10. brief anecdote

Section 5
Words for Work

In Section 5 you will learn to understand and use some words commonly used in several business areas. Lessons 26 through 35 will cover terms related to the following areas: employment, sales, marketing, accounting, finance, business computing, the Internet, leadership and group input, and shipping. These are terms that you will encounter on the job, reading work documents, in news and magazine articles, and even in your personal life. Even terms that are not directly related to your specific job are helpful—they help you understand the "big picture" of the business environment.

IMPORTANT

The lessons in Section 5 present words in the context of a work-related paragraph—a portion of a memo, notice, advertisement, or other document. The key to learning and remembering the terms in these lessons is to try to determine their meaning from the way they are used in context. Review the strategies you learned in Section 1, "Clues from Context," and use those strategies in these lessons.

Following each sample work-related document is a set of preview questions ("What Do You Know?"). Read the text containing the target words and then answer the questions. The answer to each question ("How Did You Do?") contains an explanation of the answer and the target term. Be sure to read these explanations. The definitions of the target words and phrases are given in a box at the end of each section. Read the definitions and use them to review the lesson before completing the "Working with Words" section at the end of each lesson.

WHAT DO YOU KNOW?

MULTIPLE CHOICE

Circle the letter next to the answer that best completes the sentence.

1. The business owners received the invoice for $652.00, but decided to _____ payment for 90 days.
   - (a) reimburse
   - (b) defer
   - (c) disburse
   - (d) accrue

2. Better Bikes Company _____ its bikes as being the fastest, lightest, sturdiest bikes available.
   - (a) segmented
   - (b) wholesaled
   - (c) differentiated
   - (d) manufactured

3. Please _____ payment before August 14.
   - (a) remit
   - (b) revoke
   - (c) accrue
   - (d) accumulate

4. The accounting department processed a check to _____ Charles for the expenses of his last business trip.
   - (a) reimburse
   - (b) reinstate
   - (c) intestate
   - (d) disperse

WORD SELECTION

Circle the word or phrase that best completes the sentence.

1. George used a (spider / search engine) on the Internet to find information on those vitamins.

2. The company's database file on last year's customers contains 11,430 (modems / records).

3. The city's planning commission will meet at 6:00 Friday evening for a (brainstorming / consensus) session about the proposed park.

4. The local (cartage / commodity) company will pick up the machines and deliver them across town.

HOW DID YOU DO?

Multiple Choice: (1) b; (2) c; (3) a; (4) a

Word Selection: (1) search engine; (2) records; (3) brainstorming; (4) cartage

Employment

This lesson concerns words related to employment that are common to most companies. Many businesses have a *personnel* department. A personnel or *human resources* department handles job searches, processes applications, conducts interviews, and manages employee *benefits*, such as vacation records, health insurance, and life insurance. Some human resources departments also arrange for employee training, or employee development. The terms presented in this lesson are ones that you will encounter in dealing with a human resources department, in looking for employment, and in reading job ads or company policy manuals.

COMPENSATION

Full-Time Delivery Drivers Wanted

No weekend routes. Compensation commensurate with experience. Send employment history to Garza's Flowers, Attention: Human Resources Department.

WHAT DO YOU KNOW?

Circle T or F to indicate whether each of the following statements is true or false.

T F   1. The human resources department at Garza's Flowers will probably review the applications and recommend or hire someone for the job.

T F   2. Pay is probably better for someone with more experience or better experience.

T F   3. Someone who has little experience would probably be paid less than someone who has had more experience.

HOW DID YOU DO?

1. True. Reviewing applications and recommending or hiring applicants for jobs are functions of human resources departments.

2. True. *Commensurate* means "in proper proportion." *Compensation* refers to the pay and benefits an employee receives for doing a job. The phrase "compensation commensurate with experience" indicates that the salary or wages for a job will depend on the experience of the applicant. Someone with more related experience will be paid more than a person who has less experience.

3. True. See the explanation for question 2.

TERMS RELATED TO COMPENSATION

human resources or personnel department   the department in a business that manages the employment of its workers

compensation   payment; in employment, compensation includes salary, wages, and benefits such as vacation time or health insurance

commensurate   in proper proportion; fitting

NEGOTIATION AND DISCRIMINATION

Wanted: Qualified Person to Help Customers Select Furniture

Must have interior decorating experience. Salary negotiable. Great compensation package. Apply at Isabel's Interiors. Isabel's is an Equal Opportunity Employer and does not discriminate for reasons of race, creed, color, or gender.

WHAT DO YOU KNOW?

Circle the letter of the phrase that best completes each sentence.

1. The pay for this job (a) is very high; (b) is very low; (c) is open to discussion; (d) depends upon experience.
2. Isabel's Interiors (a) hires only women; (b) hires only minorities; (c) does not decide whom to hire based on their race; (d) hires many people.
3. The person hired for this job will probably (a) be a minority; (b) not be a minority; (c) receive vacation, health, or other benefits; (d) *not* have experience.

HOW DID YOU DO?

1. (c). The pay is *negotiable*—that is, open to discussion. The pay could also depend on experience, but the ad does not provide that information.
2. (c). We know from the ad that Isabel's does not *discriminate* for reasons of race, creed, color, or gender. *Discriminate* in this context means to act or make decisions with bias. Therefore, answers (a) and (b) cannot be correct. The ad gives no information that would lead us to believe that Isabel's hires many people.
3. (c). *Compensation* means pay and benefits. Since the ad promises a good *compensation package*, we can interpret this to mean that workers receive something more than just wages.

TERMS RELATED TO NEGOTIATION AND DISCRIMINATION

negotiate   discuss with another person in order to reach an agreement

negotiable   may be discussed; open to negotiation

discriminate   act toward someone with bias or prejudice

equal opportunity employer   a business that employs workers without regard to race, creed, color, or gender

JOB PERFORMANCE

Employee Wanted

New, high-tech firm has immediate opening for versatile individual to do word processing and answer telephones. Applicants must be proficient in at least two word-processing programs and like to act on own initiative. Competence in other computer applications a plus. Send resume to this paper, Box J.

WHAT DO YOU KNOW?

Circle T or F to indicate whether each of the following statements is true or false.

T F   1. The firm wants someone who writes poetry.

T F   2. Applicants must know something about two word-processing programs.

T F   3. The person in this job will be closely supervised and directed.

T F   4. The firm will give extra consideration to someone who knows and can work with other computer programs as well.

HOW DID YOU DO?

1. False. The firm wants a *versatile* person. A *versatile* person is someone who has skills in several different areas, but not necessarily poetry.

2. False. *Proficient* means highly skilled. The ad indicates that applicants must be *proficient*—that is, highly skilled—in two word-processing programs.

3. False. The firm wants someone with *initiative*—that is, someone who is a self-starter. Therefore, the person will probably not be closely supervised and directed, but given more independence.

4. True. The ad says that *competence* in other computer applications is "a plus." *Competence* means "ability," so people who know other computer programs will be viewed more positively.

TERMS RELATED TO JOB PERFORMANCE

competence   ability

versatile   having many different types of ability or uses

to have initiative   to act without instruction; self-starting

proficient   expert; having a high level of skill

TERMINATION

Employee Notice

Due to a lack of customers, our firm has lost money four months in a row. Unfortunately, this makes it necessary to terminate the employment of several people working for our company. These employees have not yet been identified, but the decisions will be based on seniority. We assure you that anyone who is discharged for these reasons will be given a letter of recommendation as well as generous severance pay. We are very sorry that this action has become necessary.

WHAT DO YOU KNOW?

Circle the letter of the phrase that best completes each sentence.

1. Several employees will (a) be sent to work in the stock terminal; (b) be promoted; (c) be fired.
2. Employees will not be fired who (a) are old; (b) have children; (c) have worked for the firm the most years.
3. Employees will receive severance pay (a) if they have lost a finger or hand on the job; (b) if they have worked for the firm the longest period of time; (c) if they are discharged from their job.

HOW DID YOU DO?

1. (c). The notice indicates the need to *terminate* the employment of several persons. To *terminate* means "to end." In familiar, casual language, the employees will be "fired."
2. (c). *Seniority* refers to length of employment. Employees hired the earliest have the most seniority. The announcement says that the decisions will be based on seniority. Employees will be *kept* who have the most seniority.
3. (c). *Severance* is a word similar to *terminate*. *Severance pay* is an amount of money given to individuals who are terminated from a job.

TERMS RELATED TO TERMINATION

terminate   end or put a stop to, as to discharge from a job

retention   keeping employees over a period of time

severance pay   an amount of money sometimes paid to an individual being discharged or laid off from his or her job

seniority   priority due to length of employment

Working with Words

MULTIPLE CHOICE

Circle the letter next to the answer that best completes the sentence. Use your knowledge of context clues, prefixes, and roots to help you decide.

1. Josephine received an increase in _____ after a year on the job.
   (a) personnel
   (b) commensuration
   (c) compensation
   (d) initiative

2. The salary for that job is _____.
   (a) severance
   (b) deficient
   (c) proficient
   (d) negotiable

3. Mr. Morrison lacks _____; he continually needs direction.
   (a) a map
   (b) compensation
   (c) initiative
   (d) opportunity

4. Ms. Ely received _____ pay when the company terminated her job.
   (a) severance
   (b) commensurate
   (c) back
   (d) retention

5. The firm's employees had all worked there more than five years. This was considered to be a very good rate of _____.
   (a) compensation
   (b) initiative
   (c) retention
   (d) personnel

6. You will need to be interviewed by the _____ department.
   (a) compensation
   (b) initiative
   (c) retention
   (d) personnel

7. That firm has no minorities and has been accused of _____.
   (a) recrimination
   (b) initiation
   (c) discrimination
   (d) retention

8. Mr. Gardner, a very _____ person, is valuable in many areas of the company.
   (a) discriminating
   (b) commensurate
   (c) versatile
   (d) negotiable

FIND THE MISFIT

In each group, underline the word that does not belong with the others. Then state why it doesn't belong.

1. compensation, salary, benefits, retention

2. initiative, commensurate, proportionate, fair

3. initiative, versatility, competence, personnel

4. marketing, accounting, personnel, salary

5. retention, seniority, time, race

6. bargain, negotiate, salary, discuss

7. skilled, neat, proficient, competent

8. discharge, terminate, discriminate, end

USING YOUR WORDS

Use each of the following words or phrases in a sentence that demonstrates that you understand the meaning of the word or phrase.

1. seniority

2. commensurate with

3. versatile

4. proficient in

5. discriminate against

6. terminate

7. severance pay

8. negotiable

Sales

Sales and *marketing* are important activities of most businesses. Companies must sell the products they make or the services they provide to earn the money that pays the employees and keeps the firm in business.

The sales department usually has salespeople who meet directly with customers or future customers to tell them about the firm's products and services and related matters such as price or delivery schedule. Although "self-service" types of businesses, such as department and discount stores, have become increasingly popular, most of us have still had many experiences with salespeople. Some businesses, such as real estate and insurance, rely heavily on personal sales.

Marketing covers a broad range of activities. We'll work with marketing terms in the next lesson.

In this lesson, you will become familiar with terms that are commonly used in sales situations and in talking about sales. These are ones you would use in any job related to selling. You will also encounter these words when you read magazines, newspaper articles, or books about companies and what they are doing to become more successful.

SPECIAL OFFERS

MEMORANDUM

TO: George Anderson and Sally Lee,

Account Representatives, Midwest Territory

FROM: Alice King, Vice President, Sales

SUBJECT: Spring Sales Promotion

Please send me your plan for the next sales promotion of the *Dance Your Way to Health* kits in your territory.

   Will the promotion use demonstration disks, coupons, refunds, price discounts, or other incentives to motivate individuals to buy the program?

WHAT DO YOU KNOW?

Circle T or F to indicate whether each of the following statements is true or false.

T F 1. A sales promotion is a way that a company encourages potential customers to buy its product or services.

T F 2. George and Sally are assigned to sell *Dance Your Way to Health* all over the nation.

T F 3. Incentives are amounts of money given in cents.

HOW DID YOU DO?

1. True. Sales *promotions* are activities intended to motivate customers to try or to purchase more products or services.
2. False. According to the "TO:" line, George and Sally are responsible for selling the product in the Midwest only; this is their sales *territory*.
3. False. *Incentives* are offers designed to encourage the purchase of products or services.

TERMS RELATED TO SPECIAL OFFERS

sales territory   a geographic area assigned to one or more salespeople

sales promotion   a set of activities designed to increase the trial or purchase of a product or service

incentive   an offer intended to motivate customers to buy a product or service; coupons, discounts, partial refunds, and gifts-with-purchase are examples of incentives

---

WHOLESALE AND RETAIL SALES

❧ Green Growers ❧

Mr. Sam Tobias

Daisy Distributors

Green Lake, XX

Dear Distributor:

This spring's exceptionally good weather resulted in a 10 percent

increase in our harvest of Delight Daffodils and a nearly 12 percent

increase of Bronze Irises. As a result of this season's good flower

production, we are pleased to reduce our wholesale prices by 10

percent for this year's orders. Our new wholesale prices for these

two varieties are shown below.

Delight Daffodils $4.00 per dozen stems   Minimum order: 100 dozen

Bronze Irises $6.00 per dozen stems   Minimum order: 60 dozen

Daisy Distributors

Mr. Ray Garza

Garza's Flower Shop

Blue River, XX

Dear Mr. Garza:

We are pleased to inform you that we have an exceptionally fine offer on Delight Daffodils and Bronze Irises this month. Please see our wholesale prices below and let us know how many of these two great varieties you would like to add to your flower order for next week's shipment.

Delight Daffodils   Bronze Irises

$8.00 per dozen stems $12.00 per dozen stems

Minimum order: 10 dozen   Minimum order: 6 dozen

GARZA'S FLOWER SHOP

❀ ❀ ❀ ❀ ❀ ❀ ❀ ❀ ❀

Spring is here! Nothing will welcome spring into your home better than an elegant spring arrangement from Garza's Flower Shop. Select from one of the wonderful designs on display in our shop this week, or come in for individual stems to create your own spring welcome! Our special stems this week are Delight Daffodils and Bronze Irises.

Delight Daffodils $1.20 each (or buy a dozen for $12 and save $2.40)

Bronze Iris $1.80 each (or buy a dozen for $19 and save $2.60)

Come in today! You won't find lower retail prices anywhere in the city!

WHAT DO YOU KNOW?

Circle T or F to indicate whether each of the following statements is true or false.

T F 1. Daisy Distributors buys flowers wholesale for one price and sells them wholesale for another price.

T F 2. Green Growers sells flowers retail to Daisy Distributors.

T F 3. Garza's Flower Shop sells flowers retail to consumers.

T F 4. Garza's Flower Shop sells flowers retail to distributors.

T F 5. Green Growers sells flowers wholesale and Daisy Distributors sells flowers wholesale.

HOW DID YOU DO?

Manufacturers usually sell their goods wholesale. They sell them wholesale to distributors who then sell them wholesale to retailers who then sell them retail to the ultimate purchasers. Sometimes manufacturers sell their goods wholesale directly to the retailers, without using distributors. Retailers buy goods wholesale from distributors—wholesalers—and then sell them retail, increasing the price to cover their costs plus a profit.

1. True. Daisy Distributors buys flowers in bulk from the grower at a wholesale price. Then Daisy Distributors sells those flowers to flower shops in bulk—although in somewhat smaller quantities—for the shops to resell. Daisy Distributors sells the flowers for some amount more than what they paid for them.

2. False. The grower sells flowers wholesale to the distributor.

3. True. Garza's Flower Shop is the retailer that sells to the end users or purchasers.

4. False. Garza's Flower Shop does not sell to the distributor. Garza's buys from the distributor.

5. True. The grower sells the flowers wholesale to the distributor and the distributor sells them wholesale to the retailer.

TERMS RELATED TO WHOLESALE AND RETAIL SALES

wholesale   selling in bulk, or large quantity, usually to someone or some company for purposes of reselling. Some wholesalers are middlemen or distributors who buy from the manufacturer and then sell to retailers.

retail   selling to an end user or ultimate consumer

bulk sales   sales of items in large quantity

CUSTOMER SUPPORT

SUNSHINE EQUIPMENT COMPANY

Internal Memorandum

TO: Rich Andrews, VP Sales

FROM: Rob Jones

SUBJECT: Customer Meeting with Susan Smith

Earlier this week I met with Susan Smith, the operations manager at Primary Presses Company. I used the consultative selling approach by asking her about the company's needs or problems. We discussed their need to improve the efficiency of their equipment. I suggested that they could solve their low output problem by upgrading the feeder systems rather than the entire machines. This will improve their output and save them the extremely high expense of new machines.

I gave Susan information on the model XL4073D feeders. The pamphlet entitled "Facts about Your Feeders" is our features-and-benefits analysis for this model. It includes a list of the key features of this model and outlines ways in which this particular press can save the customer's space, reduce noise levels, and add time to the day!

Other sales collaterals that I left with Susan included the company brochure emphasizing our excellent customer service and low repair record, the product description sheets for the new XL651 integrated system, and a desk calendar for next year.

I expect to follow up with this client on the 6th of next month.

WHAT DO YOU KNOW?

Circle T or F to indicate whether each of the following statements is true or false.

T F   1. Rob Jones uses consultative selling strategies to sell his company's products.
T F   2. Rob Jones tries to help solve his customers' problems.
T F   3. Saving space is an example of a feature.
T F   4. Saving space is an example of a benefit.
T F   5. Sales collaterals are junior sales representatives.

HOW DID YOU DO?

1. True. Rob Jones identified the customer's problem of low output and their need to avoid spending huge amounts of money. Then he acted like a consultant by suggesting ways to do these.
2. True. Trying to solve customers' problems is the key part of consultative selling.
3. False. "A small footprint" or "14 square inches" would be features. Saving space is the benefit.
4. True. Saving space is a benefit.
5. False. Sales collaterals are materials that support the sales of a product or service.

TERMS RELATED TO CUSTOMER SUPPORT

consultative selling   a style of selling characterized by acting as a consultant to the customer, that is, helping the customer solve problems

sales collaterals   materials that support selling, such as price lists, brochures, or calendars, tablets, pens, and other items with advertising

features-and-benefits analysis   list(s) of characteristics (features) of a product or service that help distinguish them from other products or services; lists of ways in which a product or service will help the customer, solve a problem, etc. (benefits)

PERSONAL SELLING

Interview

(Partial Transcript)

Ms. Russell, Sales Manager at Russell Machine Company: Tell me, Mr. Evans, how you see the difference between a "lead" and a "prospect" for our company.

Mr. Evans, Job Applicant: A lead is just a name or a name and contact information. A prospect is someone who has a need for your product or service and also has the resources to purchase your machines. Also, a true prospect has the authority to make the decision to buy. I'd also use another category—"qualified prospects." These are the prospects who have potential for a sale large enough to justify my spending time and other resources to sell to them.

Ms. Russell: For a company like ours, how would you go about prospecting?

Mr. Evans: For this company, I would identify prospects by getting referrals from existing customers, sending direct-mail promotions to companies that use this type of product, and making contacts at trade shows.

Ms. Russell: Why do you think you were successful at your last company?

Mr. Evans: After I have identified prospects, I do very thorough preparation and preapproach planning. By this I mean that before I contact a prospect, I study as much information about that person or company as I can obtain. I make notes on how the product meets needs that the prospect might have. And I practice my presentation before every sales call. One other thing I do is try to predict all of the objections that the prospect might have. Then I develop the best answer or information to overcome the objections. I listen to prospects very carefully because I know they often have objections or excuses to avoid making decisions.

Ms. Russell: What about closing, Mr. Evans? After all, your record is only as good as your closings.

Mr. Evans: I see the close as the process of helping people make a decision. I help by asking them to buy. Sometimes I just ask them to say yes. Other times I put a purchase agreement before them and ask them to sign it. But I always do something that helps them make the decision to buy.

WHAT DO YOU KNOW?

Circle T or F to indicate whether each of the following statements is true or false.

T F 1. A sales lead and a prospect are the same.

T F 2. Sales prospecting refers to various processes of identifying potential customers.

T F 3. In the selling process, preapproach activities are those done before prospecting.

T F 4. *Closing* refers to when a customer or future customer closes the door on a sales representative.

T F 5. Sales representatives don't have to worry about prospects' objections. Either the prospects will buy or they won't.

HOW DID YOU DO?

1. False. A lead may or may not become a prospect. A prospect is a person or company that has a need for the product or service, the resources to purchase it, and the authority to make the decision.

2. True. Prospecting consists of various activities used to identify potential customers or "prospects."

3. False. Preapproach activities are those done prior to actually approaching the prospect to request an appointment or make a sales presentation.

4. False. Closing refers to the process of helping a potential buyer make the decision to buy, often by asking for the business or sale.

5. False. Overcoming objections is a common part of the sales process and salespeople must develop these skills also.

TERMS RELATED TO PERSONAL SELLING

prospect   a person or company who has a need for the product or service, the resources to purchase it, and the authority to make the decision

prospecting   the process of identifying potential customers or clients

preapproach activities   the part of the selling process devoted to planning and preparation to ask for an appointment or make a sales presentation

overcoming objections   responding to a prospect's objections in such a way that the obstacles to the sale are removed

closing   helping a prospect make the decision to buy

Working with Words

FILL IN THE BLANKS

From the following list, select the word that *best fits* the meaning of each sentence and write the word in the blank space provided. Use each word only once. Use all of the words.

territories   wholesale   sales collaterals   consultative selling
prospect   retail   features-and-benefits   closing
incentive   prospecting

1. T-Mart buys t-shirts in bulk from the factory and sells them _____ to consumers in their shop.

2. A _____ analysis describes a product's characteristics and tells how it can help the purchaser.

3. _____ involves assessing needs or problems and trying to solve them.

4. The _____ that Amos George gave to his client included a booklet on how to get a home loan, an information sheet on evaluating personal creditworthiness, and a small calculator with his name and phone number printed above the display.

5. Apex Distribution Company bought their supplies of paint products from Picture Perfect Paint Manufacturing, Inc. They bought them _____.

6. Identifying potential customers is also known as _____.

7. The company divided the country into geographical _____ and then assigned two representatives to each area.

8. As an _____ to buy their cars, the automobile maker offered to include twenty tanks of free gasoline.

9. As part of her _____, Joan asked the pharmacist if she would like to order two dozen bottles of the new drug.

10. Cliff was not a good _____ for ABC Machines because he had new equipment and did not need any new machines.

FIND THE MISFIT

In each group, underline the word that does not belong with the others. Then state why it doesn't belong.

1. sales collateral, support material, product, price list

2. problem-solving, helpful, physician, consultative

3. customer, distributor, middleman, wholesaler

4. retail seller, seller to end user, manufacturer, seller to ultimate purchaser

5. wholesale, bulk, quantity, telemarketing

6. offer, cents, coupon, incentive

7. sales promotion, features and benefits, consultative selling, problem-solving

8. lead, follow, prospect, potential customer

9. closing, preapproach, preparation, planning

10. territory, prospecting, closing, preapproach planning

SHORT ANSWER

Read the following ad and answer the questions that follow it.

ATTENTION HEALTH SEEKERS!
Special from Harry's!

Lose weight and improve your physical well being without pain! Try the Carla Simpson *Dance Your Way to Health* six-step system. Start today!

Now you can buy your own *Dance Your Way to Health* kit at half of the regular retail price. Harry's Human Health Supply Shop has just received a huge shipment of complete Carla Simpson *Dance Your Way to Health* kits. We bought these kits at the manufacturer's wholesale prices, and we're passing the savings on to you!

The *Dance Your Way to Health* kits give you six full hours of videotape, including one hour of yoga instruction and four hours of dance aerobics. Tape six reviews the principles of good nutrition. The kit includes diagrams of the dance aerobics steps.

Dance Your Way to Health is the easy-to-understand, easy-to-follow health system. No heavy body chemistry textbooks to master. No impossible diets to follow. Eat whatever you like. End those embarrassing moments when that doctor's scale says you're "in the red zone."

Dance Your Way to Health offers true value for your fitness dollar. Compare our low price to what you would pay retail for other programs. You'll like what you learn.

Come in and buy today and receive absolutely free Harry's fitness progress chart. Hurry. Offer good only while supplies last, and our supplies are going fast.

1. What incentive does Harry's give readers to buy the kit soon?

2. What did Harry pay for the kits?

3. What price is Harry selling them for? Is this probably a good price for the consumers?

4. List four features of the *Dance Your Way to Health* kit.

5. List three benefits of the *Dance Your Way to Health* kit.

Marketing

In some companies, the sales and marketing work is part of the same department or division. Other companies have a separate marketing department. Whether marketing stands separate from a sales department or is part of it, it will have certain tasks and responsibilities. Here are some of them.

A marketing department is usually responsible for market research or planning activities, including the following:

- identifying the needs and preferences of potential customers

- evaluating new products or services to fill those needs

- deciding which types of customers the company should try to reach

- helping the company decide how to provide the goods and services that those buyers will purchase

After customers use the firm's goods or services, the marketing department will:

- try to find out whether the customers are satisfied

- determine whether the firm's offerings need to be increased, improved, changed, or dropped altogether

In addition, marketing departments are usually responsible for:

- advertising

- direct mail or e-mail campaigns

- the company's Web site(s)
- telemarketing
- flyers
- brochures
- catalogs
- promotions

In this lesson, you will become familiar with terms that are commonly used with regard to marketing. These terms are ones you would use in any job related to marketing. You will also encounter these words when you read magazines, newspaper articles, or books about companies and what they are doing to become more successful.

MARKET RESEARCH

Memorandum

TO: Bette Royce

FROM: Market Research Director

SUBJECT: Results of Shopper Survey

Over the past few weeks, we asked shoppers in the

UltraWorld Shopping Mall to complete a short survey

about our new line of products called "Silken Moments."

We also asked some shoppers to try the product and then

we interviewed them. The results of this market research

indicate that only one market segment will pay a

substantial premium to obtain Silken Moments lotions and

creams.

The demographics of the market segment that indicated

willingness to purchase these products include the

following: income over $80,000 per year, an average age

of 38 years, education level of two years of college or

more, and female.

WHAT DO YOU KNOW?

Circle T or F to indicate whether each of the following statements is true or false.

T F 1. One kind of market research gathers information about customers' likes and preferences, buying behaviors, and other characteristics.

T F 2. A market segment is a particular type or group of people who buy goods and services.

T F 3. Demographics is the type of art used on product packaging.

T F 4. In marketing language, a market segment is part of a grocery store.

T F 5. The market segment that would be most likely to buy Silken Moments lotions and creams is work-study students.

HOW DID YOU DO?

1. True. Other market research examines competing products, services, and companies, tests the effectiveness of advertisements or promotions, and evaluates locations for stores or offices.

2. True. A market segment is a part of the purchasing public or decision makers that have something in common. People who go sailing, travel, go to school, or earn a certain income could each be a market segment. Notice that some market segments overlap.

3. False. Demographics are statistics about groups of people. The prefix *demo-* refers to people, as in *democracy*.

4. False. A market segment is a group of customers or potential customers.

5. False. The people in the market segment most likely to buy Silken Moments products are about 38 years old and earn good incomes. These are probably not work-study students.

TERMS RELATED TO MARKET RESEARCH	

market research   information collection and analysis related to a company's customers, products or services, competitors, or advertising

market segment   a group of customers or potential customers who have an interest, need, lifestyle, or other characteristic in common

demographics   statistics that describe populations or groups of people

COMPETITION

Memorandum

TO: Feathered Friends Employees

FROM: Marketing Director

SUBJECT: Positioning

The new Feathered Friends assemble-your-own houses are positioned as high-quality, easy-to-assemble birdhouses, especially the multifamily bird condominiums. We want Feathered Friends to be the brand consumers think of when it comes to houses for any kind of bird—the name as familiar to bird lovers as Broadway is to theater lovers. Feathered Friends will be the household word for birdhouses.

Our main competitor is Brown's Bedrooms for Birds. Our houses will be differentiated from Brown's houses by being buildable in half the time. Also, our houses are much better quality.

Up until now, our whole company has been known for quality, and we shall make sure that the Feathered Friends birdhouses will continue this positioning. People know that Brown's Bedrooms means

cheap. We want to be sure that we do not get that reputation.

Please remember that Feathered Friends means "Quality for Birds" in

everything you do!

WHAT DO YOU KNOW?

Circle T or F to indicate whether each of the following statements is true or false.

T F   1. To differentiate means to distinguish one product or company from another.

T F   2. A competitor to Feathered Friends is Broadway.

T F   3. Feathered Friends birdhouses' positioning is about six feet above the ground.

T F   4. Feathered Friends wants to be a brand name.

T F   5. Positioning refers to how something is perceived by the marketplace. Differentiation is how something is different from other products or services.

HOW DID YOU DO?

1. True. Differentiation means how something is different or how people perceive it as different.

2. False. Feathered Friends' competitors are other companies that sell birdhouses.

3. False. In marketing, *positioning* refers to the position something holds in the minds of the buyers or the public. Feathered Friends wants to claim the position of "high-quality and easy to assemble."

4. True. Becoming a brand name means becoming an extremely familiar name, and that name should carry some meaning. Since brand names are so widely recognized, they tend to sell more.

5. True. Positioning and differentiation are similar in some ways, but they are not always exactly the same.

TERMS RELATED TO COMPETITION

brand, branding   to give something a broadly recognized, distinctive identity; products, services, and companies can all be "branded"; examples include Kleenex, Microsoft, IBM, Coke, and FedEx

positioning   also called market position; how a company, product, or service is perceived by people in the relevant market; reputation

company differentiation   how a company is distinguished from similar companies

product differentiation   how a product is made distinctive or different from other products; how it is made special for a market segment or group

competitor   a company that sells a similar product to the same market segment as another company; for example, Ford Motors and General Motors are competitors; Fords and Chevrolets are competing products

Working with Words

FILL IN THE BLANKS

From the following list, select the word that *best fits* the meaning of each sentence and write the word in the blank space provided. Use each word only once. Use all of the words.

segment	branding	differentiation
demographics	research	competitors

1. A group of customers who share an interest, need, or other attribute is called a market _____.

2. A company's market _____ includes its examination of customers' needs and priorities.

3. A product whose name and characteristics are very well known is said to have _____.

4. United Airlines and Northwest Airlines are _____.

5. _____ refers to statistical information about a population or group of people.

6. Companies use product _____ to distinguish their product or service from other products or services.

FIND THE MISFIT

In each group, underline the word that does not belong with the others. Then state why it doesn't belong.

1. differentiate, distinguish, stand out, sell

2. shared characteristics, market segment, product features, buyer types

3. household term, company name, high recognition, brand

4. group characteristics, demographics, statistics, democracy

5. partner, rival, competitor, adversary

SHORT ANSWER

Read the following ad and answer the questions that follow it.

> **Attention Oregon Parents!**
>
> Help your children learn mathematics the fun way—with *Numbers On!*, the new math instructional software that guarantees success for every child.
>
> Your children can have fun mastering math concepts while conquering outer space or discovering lost civilizations. Learners apply math to motivating, creative problems involving time and space.
>
> *Numbers On!* offers true value for your educational dollar. Our low price is half the price of *Math Crunch* or *Math Master*. Compare today— and you'll soon order *Numbers On!*

1. Name two competitors of *Numbers On!*

2. What market segment does this ad target? Describe the people this ad is trying to reach.

3. How is *Numbers On!* differentiated from its competitors?

4. What do we know about the *Numbers On!* positioning?

USING YOUR WORDS

Use each of the following words or phrases in a sentence that demonstrates that you understand the meaning of the word or phrase.

1. market segment

2. product differentiation

3. competitor

4. demographics

5. market research

6. brand

Accounting

Accounting is a critical business function. An accounting department is usually responsible for paying the firm's bills and for billing its customers. Accounting employees check customers' credit and collect the money owed to the company. Employees' pay and pay records are managed by accounting. Additionally, the accounting department is responsible for budgeting, tax preparation, reporting on the finances of the firm, and financial planning. Businesses, even small ones, generally have an accounting department, and the terms used in accounting are, therefore, very useful to know. You will encounter finance and accounting terms in sending out invoices or paying bills, in keeping records of expenses or sales or cash, and in checking budgets or financial documents.

PAYING BILLS

The Tree Doctor

4092 Eighth St., Riverside, CA 9250X (909) 555-4068

February 18, 200X

Horizon Recreation Village

Accounting Department

4041 Walnut Street

Riverside, CA 9250X

Dear Sir/Madam:

Four months ago, we sent you an invoice for trimming your trees. Shortly thereafter, your accounts payable division indicated that you needed to defer payment for 60 days due to a business slowdown.

The 60 days, and more, have now passed. Please remit payment immediately. Our accounts receivable department will be expecting your check within seven days.

Thank you for your immediate attention to this matter.

Sincerely,

Rosella Springer

Rosella Springer

Accounts Receivable Manager

WHAT DO YOU KNOW?

Circle the word in parentheses that best completes each sentence.

1. Our (payables / receivables) department would like to receive your payment as soon as possible.
2. Your (payables / receivables) department has not sent payment.
3. (Remit / Permit) payment immediately. Do not (defer / refer) payment to a later date.
4. We are sending the (invoice / manual) for our services. Please pay it within seven days.

HOW DID YOU DO?

1. receivables. *Receivables* departments receive payments. They also send out invoices and statements.
2. payables. *Payables* departments pay invoices.
3. remit; defer. To *remit* payment is to send it; to *defer* it is to delay it.
4. invoice. An *invoice* is a bill asking for payment.

TERMS RELATED TO PAYING BILLS

invoice   list of items or services along with their prices, shipping, and other costs, indicating an amount owed by the customer; a bill

remit   send payment

defer   delay

payable   owed by a company or individual; an amount to be paid

receivable   owed to a company or individual; an amount to be received or collected

---

BUDGETING

The Tree Doctor

Internal Memorandum

TO: Yoshi K., Accounting Clerk

FROM: Art Duarte, Accounting Manager

SUBJECT: Budget Preparation

DATE: June 25, 200X

When you prepare the company budget for next year, please note the following:

1. You need to allocate $5,000 to the computer equipment fund.

2. We will allow the building renovation expenses to accrue for
   six months.

3. Prorate payment for the new furniture evenly over the year.

4. Overhead expenses include rent, furniture, utilities, and
   computer services.

5. Charge salaries, telephone, and other expenses to specific
   projects.

WHAT DO YOU KNOW?

Circle T or F to indicate whether each of the following statements is true or false.

T F   1. The company will pay for the building renovation before the work is done.
T F   2. The company plans to make equal monthly payments for the furniture.
T F   3. The firm will not have money for computer equipment this year.
T F   4. The expenses for power are part of overhead.

HOW DID YOU DO?

1. False. The company will allow the expenses for this work to *accrue,* or accumulate, for six months.
2. True. The company plans to *prorate,* or distribute proportionately, the amount it owes.
3. False. The firm *allocated,* or set aside, funds for computer equipment.
4. True. *Overhead* consists of general expenses that are not charged to specific projects.

TERMS RELATED TO BUDGETING	
prorate	distribute proportionately
allocate	set aside or designate funds for a special purpose
accrue	accumulate
overhead	expenses that cannot be charged directly to specific activities or projects; examples of overhead expenses are rent and utilities

REMUNERATION

The Tree Doctor

4092 Eighth St., Riverside, CA 9250X (909) 555-4068

November 4, 200X

Dr. Anthony Argos, Tree Surgeon

14041 Terracina Drive

Riverside, CA 9250X

Dear Dr. Argos:

Thank you for your inquiry about being a consultant to our firm. We do use consultants from time to time and will be happy to add your name to our list.

We pay consultants on a per diem basis, and the amount of the remuneration is equal to that paid by other tree services. We also reimburse your expenses for materials or chemicals you purchase to test a tree.

   We appreciate your interest in our company.

Sincerely,

Alice Adams

Alice Adams

President

WHAT DO YOU KNOW?

Circle the word in parentheses that best completes each sentence.

1. The Tree Doctor pays consultants by the (day / hour).
2. The Tree Doctor pays consultants (more than / the same as) other tree services.
3. The Tree Doctor (deducts / pays) a consultant's expenses.

HOW DID YOU DO?

1. day. The Tree Doctor's consultants are paid a *per diem,* or daily, rate.
2. the same as. According to the letter, *remuneration,* or pay, is the same as paid by other tree services.
3. pays. The Tree Doctor *reimburses* expenses. To reimburse is to replace money that has been spent by someone for expenses.

TERMS RELATED TO REMUNERATION

reimburse   to pay back an amount that has been spent

remuneration   payment for

per diem   per day; daily

BALANCE SHEETS

The Tree Doctor Buys Acorn Industries

The Tree Doctor revealed today that it has purchased Acorn Industries. Acorn's balance sheet shows that its assets, especially the oak farm, make it a solid purchase. Acorn's liabilities of about $50,000 consist primarily of money Acorn owes in back taxes . . .

WHAT DO YOU KNOW?

Circle T or F to indicate whether each of the following statements is true or false.

T F   1. Acorn Industries is broke.

T F   2. A liability is the ability to give false financial information.

T F   3. A balance sheet reports the financial health of a company.

HOW DID YOU DO?

1. False. They own an oak farm, at least, and it is an *asset.*
2. False. A *liability* is money owed by a firm.
3. True.

TERMS RELATED TO BALANCE SHEETS

assets   the property, cash, amounts due, and so on owned by a company

liabilities   the debts, amounts owed, and so on of a company

balance sheet   a report showing the dollar value of a firm's assets and liabilities at a particular point in time

Working with Words

MULTIPLE CHOICE

Circle the letter next to the answer that best completes the sentence. Use your knowledge of context clues, prefixes, and roots to help you decide.

1. We would like to _____ payment for 30 days; a check will be mailed to you at that time.
   - (a) reimburse
   - (b) reconcile
   - (c) defer
   - (d) defrost

2. Please _____ payment as soon as possible.
   - (a) refuse
   - (b) remit
   - (c) commit
   - (d) defer

3. Our _____ department will send you a check for the amount the company owes you.
   - (a) payables
   - (b) ledgers
   - (c) receivables
   - (d) invoice

4. Please _____ the office rent so that the company pays only for the days it occupied the building.
   - (a) pay
   - (b) remit
   - (c) prorate
   - (d) accrue

5. The budget committee _____ funds specifically for upgrading the computer system.
   - (a) allocated
   - (b) balanced
   - (c) prorated
   - (d) reimbursed

6. Mr. Yee asked the firm to _____ his travel expenses as soon as possible.
   - (a) renovate
   - (b) defer
   - (c) reimburse
   - (d) reform

7. Ms. Redwing indicated that the _____ offered to her for completing the project was adequate.
   - (a) remuneration
   - (b) asset
   - (c) invoice
   - (d) debit

8. Does the firm have more _____ or liabilities?
   - (a) balances
   - (b) assets
   - (c) accounting
   - (d) marketing

FIND THE MISFIT

In each group, underline the word that does not belong with the others. Then state why it doesn't belong.

1. pay, accrue, remit, reimburse

2. remuneration, reimbursement, compensation, reconciliation

3. asset, allocate, prorate, accrue

4. balance sheet, liability, asset, receivable

USING YOUR WORDS

Use each of the following words or phrases in a sentence that demonstrates that you understand the meaning of the word or phrase.

1. remit payment

2. allocate funds for

3. payables clerk

4. overdue invoices

5. balance sheet

6. remuneration for

7. prorate the amount

8. request reimbursement for

9. overhead

10. asset

Finance

This chapter will familiarize you with some basic terms related to two important areas of business: loans and investments. The terms are ones that you will encounter in your personal finances as well as in business.

LOANS

Paula's Precision Book Printing Company has decided to add binding the books to its services. Since the binding equipment is quite expensive, Paula borrows the money to purchase it. Paula borrows $20,000 from Ocean Vista Bank. To loan her the money, the bank will charge Paula interest at the rate of 6 percent. In addition, Paula pledges the printing presses that she owns as collateral. This means that if she doesn't make her payments, the bank can take her printing presses.

Promissory Note

Ocean Vista, California May 17, 20XX

I promise to pay Ocean Vista Bank (Obligee) the principal sum of

twenty thousand and no/100 ----- dollars plus interest at the rate of

6 percent. Payments will be made in installments of one thousand and

<u>no/100</u> ----- dollars on the <u>first</u> day of each month beginning <u>July 1,</u>

<u>200X,</u> continuing until said principal and interest have been paid.

As collateral, Paula's Precision Book Printing Company pledges its three

Vandenberg printing presses. If any installment is not paid when due, Ocean Vista

Bank may take possession of the three printing presses.

Paula Parker

Borrower (Obligor)

WHAT DO YOU KNOW?

Circle T or F to indicate whether each of the following statements is true or false.

T F   1. Paula Parker is an obligor.
T F   2. The term *collateral* means printing presses.
T F   3. The term *principal* refers to the amount borrowed.
T F   4. *Rate of interest* refers to a percentage.
T F   5. An obligee owes money to an obligor.
T F   6. A promissory note is an agreement regarding a loan.

HOW DID YOU DO?

1. True. Paula Parker is borrowing the money. An obligor is someone who is obligated to repay a loan. An obligor is a debtor.
2. False. Collateral refers to some property that a borrower pledges to protect the lender's investment. If the borrower does not meet the terms of the loan, the lender can take the collateral. The collateral may be any property that the lender is willing to accept as security for the loan.
3. True. Principal refers to the amount of money borrowed.
4. True. Rate refers to a percentage.
5. False. An obligor owes the money to the obligee. The obligor is the one who owes.
6. True. A promissory note is an agreement about a loan, its amount, rate of interest, and terms of payment.

TERMS RELATED TO LOANS

principal   the amount borrowed

rate   in this context, the percent that is used to calculate the interest on a loan.

interest   payment for the use of someone else's money; the dollar amount of the interest is usually calculated as a percentage of the money borrowed; the percentage is called the rate

collateral   property pledged by a borrower to protect the interests of the lender; if the borrower does not meet the terms of the loan, the lender may take the collateral

promissory note   an agreement between a borrower and a lender that states that the borrower will repay a certain loan amount at a certain rate of interest; any terms of the loan are also stated, such as the amount of the payments and when they are due; the borrower and the lender both sign the note

obligee   the party to a promissory note who is the lender of the money

obligor   the party to a promissory note who is the borrower of the money

---

INVESTMENTS

Individuals, companies, and governments all invest money, hoping that the investment will earn them more money. Investments may be large sums of money, or they may be quite modest. Stocks, bonds, and real estate are examples of investments. Depositing any amount in a savings account that pays some rate of interest is an investment. Investments may be relatively safe, as in the savings account example, or they may be risky. As a general rule, risky investments have potential for greater rewards—but also for greater losses.

Pig House Investment Reaps Large Profits

NEW YORK—John Rumpole announced today that his investment of $5 million in a company that manufactures shelters for pigs has made a sizable profit. "The return on this investment has been much greater than expected," commented Rumpole. "Due to an extremely harsh winter in the key pig farming regions of the world, the shelters were in very high demand. Business was excellent!"

In addition to the pig houses, eccentric Rumpole's portfolio includes investments in Alaskan icebergs, stock in a tapioca company, stock in a deep-sea shipwreck recovery company, and agate mines in Colorado.

WHAT DO YOU KNOW?

Circle T or F to indicate whether each of the following statements is true or false.

T F   1. People usually invest money with the hope or expectation that it will result in more money.

T F   2. A return on an investment means that the investment was rejected and sent back to the investor.

T F   3. All the investments of a person or company or government taken together are called a briefcase.

T F   4. Rumpole should not have invested in shelters for pigs. This was a bad investment.

HOW DID YOU DO?

1. True. An investment is usually made to reap some profit.

2. False. A return on an investment is the profit made on it. Often the return on an investment is expressed as an annual percentage rate.

3. False. The combined investments held by a person, company, or government are called a portfolio.

4. False. Rumpole's investment in the pig shelters made money for Rumpole. The return on the investment was good.

TERMS RELATED TO INVESTMENTS

investment   the outlay of money usually for income or profit

return on investment   the income or profit made on an investment; often called *ROI* for short

portfolio   combined holdings of stocks, bonds, commodities, real estate, and other investments

Working with Words

WORD SELECTION

Circle the word or phrase in parentheses that best completes each sentence.

1. JKL Cleaners borrowed $8,000 from the local bank to buy new electric racks for their finished work. The $8,000 is the (principal / interest) of the loan.
2. JKL Cleaners and the bank signed a (collateral / promissory note).
3. As (obligor / obligee), JKL Cleaners owes money.
4. As (obligor / obligee), the bank will receive the loaned money back from JKL Cleaners.
5. JKL Cleaners will probably pay (collateral / interest) to the bank.
6. The bank asked JKL Cleaners to pledge its cleaning equipment as (collateral / interest).
7. Mary Case has 100 shares of IBM stock, $12,000 worth of municipal bonds, and several commercial real estate investments in her (return on investment / portfolio).
8. Madison Kelly bought $5,000 worth of stock in E. M. Industries, expecting to earn about 8 percent back. The $5,000 is Kelly's (return on investment / investment).

FIND THE MISFIT

In each group, underline the word that does not belong with the others. Then state why it doesn't belong.

1. obligor, lender, debtor, borrower

2. promissory note, agreement, contract, money

3. security, property, investment, collateral

4. lender, obligee, debtor, loan maker

5. obligors, investment, stocks, savings

6. interest, amount borrowed, amount loaned, principal

7. portfolio, return on investment, money earned, profit

8. real estate, bonds, interest, investment

USING YOUR WORDS

Use each of the following words or phrases in a sentence that demonstrates that you understand the meaning of the word or phrase.

1. promissory note

2. principal

3. rate

4. obligor

5. collateral

6. obligee

7. return on investment

8. portfolio

Business Computing

In this "information age," more information is created and communicated, and more quickly, than most of us could have imagined only a few years ago. Most businesses today, even small ones, use some form of computer technology for information processing and communications. Office workers use *word-processing* programs to prepare a wide range of documents—from simple memos and letters to complex reports and newsletters. *Data-processing* programs, such as spreadsheet and database programs, are used for storage and analysis of various types of information: to maintain financial records; to analyze company finances; to monitor inventories of goods, purchase orders, and shipping records; to store employee and payroll information; and to perform many other tasks.

Familiarity with the basic terms of information processing and communication is essential for working in today's businesses. In this lesson you will learn to use some common terms in this area. In Lessons 32 and 33, you will learn terminology related to the Internet.

EQUIPMENT

Memo to all Office Staff

The office equipment will be moved next Monday

evening. When you report to your new workstation on

237

Tuesday, please check to see that your computer equipment is set up and working properly. Check all *hardware*, including your *peripherals*, to make sure everything is properly connected. Each workstation is now equipped with a printer and a scanner.

Test your *software* programs, especially your word-processing, database, and spreadsheet applications, and report any problems to the IT (information technologies) department. Also, check to make sure that you have not lost any information from your data files. Since we completed a full *backup* prior to the move, we can restore any missing or corrupted files.

In the new office, all computers are electronically connected to a *network,* so you will be able to share *applications* and data.

WHAT DO YOU KNOW?

Read the preceding memo. Using context clues, determine the meaning of each italicized word. Then, from the following list, select the word that best completes each sentence and write the word in the blank space provided. Check the definition to verify your answer.

applications	peripherals	hardware
network	backup	software

1. Susan created _____ files so that she could restore her important data if her computer failed.

2. Henry is an expert on spreadsheet and word-processing _____ or _____ programs.

3. _____ include various things to attach to a computer, such as printers and scanners.

4. An important advantage of a _____ is that programs and data can be easily shared.

5. A computer is _____.

HOW DID YOU DO?

1. backup. A backup file is a copy of a file.

2. applications; software. Applications are the types of software programs that a computer uses to accomplish tasks such as word processing, financial reports, games, and other activities.

3. peripherals. The word *peripheral* means "outer" or "around the edges." So things that attach to a computer rather than being inside it are called peripherals.

4. network. Programs and data can be shared by users of a network because the users' computers are linked together.

5. hardware. Computers and peripherals are called hardware. *Software* refers to programs or sets of commands that make the computer do things.

TERMS RELATED TO EQUIPMENT

applications   programs that a computer uses to accomplish tasks such as word processing, financial reports, games, and so on

backup   a copy of a file

hardware   computers and peripherals

network   computers linked together to share applications or data

peripherals   the things that attach to a computer (whether by cables, infra-red, or other connections) such as a printer, scanner, or mouse

software   the programs or sets of instructions or commands that make computers do things

WORD PROCESSING

Memo to Newsletter Staff

For the headlines of the next issue of the company newsletter, please use a *font* that is bold and clean; I want the headlines to stand out. Also, please *justify* the columns only on the left; leave the right side of the columns ragged.

A cover letter should be mailed with the newsletter to everyone in the company at his or her home. Can we insert each name and address from the employee list into a standard letter? Do we have the capability to perform this *merge*?

WHAT DO YOU KNOW?

Read the preceding memo. Using context clues, determine the meaning of each italicized word. Then, from the following list, select the word that best fits each definition and write the word in the blank space provided. Check the definition to verify your answer.

font   justify   merge

1. The appearance of printed letters and numbers: _____

2. Combine: _____

3. Make even along a left or right hand margin (or both): _____

HOW DID YOU DO?

1. font. A font is the particular design of a set of letters and numbers. Examples include Times Roman, Arial, and Courier.

2. merge. When you enter a highway or freeway and drive into and along with a line of traffic, the process is called a merge. The same is true for putting data from two or more files together . . . the process is called a merge.

3. justify. In this context, justify means to make even along one or both side margins.

TERMS RELATED TO WORD PROCESSING
font   a particular style and size of type
justify   make even along a margin (*left* or *right*) or along both margins (*full*)
merge   combine; commonly used in word processing to refer to combining information on a mailing list with the text of a letter

SPREADSHEETS

MEMO TO THE STAFF

Mr. McGee used his spreadsheet application to prepare a company budget. The *spreadsheet* shown below presents Mr. McGee's budget estimates for the next three months. Note that the *cells* in the *row* across the top of the spreadsheet show the *column* titles (the months) and the cells in the column on the left show the row titles (the budget categories). The cells in the body of the spreadsheet show the dollar estimates.

Please note that the spreadsheet application has totaled the estimates for each month. These totals are shown in the bottom row. The application has also totaled the estimates for the three expense categories. These totals are shown in the column on the right. The grand total for the three months is shown in the bottom right-hand cell.

Budget Estimates				
	APRIL	MAY	JUNE	TOTAL
Salaries	$30,000	$30,000	$32,000	$92,000
Equipment and Supplies	$2,500	$2,250	$2,800	$7,550
Overhead	$6,000	$6,000	$6,000	$18,000
Total	$38,500	$38,250	$40,800	$117,550

WHAT DO YOU KNOW?

Read the preceding memo. Using context clues, determine the meaning of each italicized word. Then, from the following list, select the word that best completes each sentence and write the word in the blank space provided. Check the definition to verify your answer.

spreadsheet   row   column   cell

1. The area in Mr. McGee's budget that contains the number $2,800 is called a

   _____.

2. All of the salaries and their total are shown in one _____.

3. All of the expenses for April are shown in one _____.

4. _____ refers to the format of Mr. McGee's budget presentation and the application that made it.

HOW DID YOU DO?

1. cell. Actually, each little square in the table is called a cell.
2. row. The salaries and their total are listed horizontally—*across* the table—in a row.
3. column. The expenses for April are listed vertically—down the table—in a column.
4. spreadsheet. Mr. McGee's data is laid out in a spreadsheet format. Spreadsheets can be paper with the lines laid out in a grid, or spreadsheets can be electronic, that is, computer applications.

TERMS RELATED TO SPREADSHEETS

spreadsheet   a table consisting of rows and columns; computer spreadsheet applications can do much more than simply display text and numbers; they can perform sophisticated calculations defined by users

row   horizontal section; an area going across the sheet

column   vertical section; an area going down the sheet

cell   in a spreadsheet, the area where a row and a column intersect

---

DATABASES

MEMO TO THE STAFF (continued)

The firm's *database program* manages a wealth of data concerning the company. An important *database file* you should know about is the customer order file. This file contains a *record* for each purchase. Each purchase record contains four *fields*—customer, item, price, and date of the purchase. Those of you in sales should find this file extremely useful for your planning and reporting.

WHAT DO YOU KNOW?

Read the preceding memo. Using context clues, determine the meaning of each italicized word. Then, from the following list, select the word or phrase that best completes each sentence and write the word or phrase in the blank space provided.

database files   fields   records   database program

1. Inside a database file are _____ that contain related information such as a customer's orders or an employee's pay and deductions.

2. Records are composed of _____.

3. We use a _____ called DataKeep.

4. Facts and figures are contained in _____.

HOW DID YOU DO?

1. records. For example, your school probably keeps all your course grades in your student record, and your bank keeps a record of all the transactions for your checking account. A single order could be a record.

2. fields. For example, a record of an order for a sweater might include fields for style, color, size, date of order, customer name, customer address, date shipped, price of item, tax, weight, shipping, and other related information.

3. database program. The application that computers use to enter, sort, retrieve, analyze, and report the information in a database is a database program.

TERMS RELATED TO DATABASES

database file   sometimes called just a *database*; a collection of data that can be organized in various ways

database program   a software application that allows a user to enter and organize data, retrieve it, and report it

record   part of a database file containing information about one transaction, one employee, one customer, and so on

field   part of a record in which a particular type of data is stored, such as name, date, size, and so on

Working with Words

WORD SELECTION

Circle the word in parentheses that best completes each sentence.

1. Matt designed the (record / spreadsheet) so that the rows showed the type of product and the columns listed the days of the week.

2. How many (programs / records) are in that file?

3. How many (cells / peripherals) are in that spreadsheet?

4. Headlines are usually printed in a larger (font / justification) than the body of the information.

5. (Databases / Records) allow users to organize information in various ways.

6. Enter the amount in the (record / field) called "price."

7. Gail has very good (word processing / justification) skills; she will be able to produce your letter quickly.

8. Is your computer system connected to a (field / network)?

FIND THE MISFIT

In each group, underline the word that does not belong with the others. Then state why it doesn't belong.

1. font, justification, word processing, network

2. database, records, hardware, information

3. individuals, spreadsheet, cells, rows

4. word processing, database, document, letter

5. hardware, mouse, application, monitor

6. software, application, workstation, program

7. spreadsheet, peripheral, database, word processing

8. hardware, software, peripheral, monitor

USING YOUR WORDS

Use each of the following words or phrases in a sentence that demonstrates that you understand the meaning of the word or phrase.

1. spreadsheet

2. word processing

3. database

4. spreadsheet cells

5. maintain records

6. modem

7. left justify

8. network

9. font

10. merge

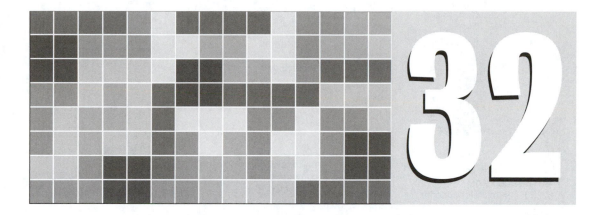

The Internet 1

The beginning of the twenty-first century saw what some have called the "invasion of the Internet." Indeed, the "information superhighway" has changed many aspects of business life, education, and everyday living forever. While inventive youth, technology wizards, and venture capitalists were quick to enter the fray in cyberspace, skeptics prophesied that the Web would crumble and leave Internet marketing, information, and investments in a shambles. The final count will probably not be seen for a long while, but e-mail and the Web are definitely here to stay. In this lesson and the one that follows, you will become familiar with a selection of the terms that have entered our language since the Web became so accessible and easy to use.

E-MAIL

Figure 32.1 shows the life of an e-mail message, from its composition by the e-mail sender to its receipt by the e-mail recipient. Trace the path of the message. Notice the various pieces of equipment involved, services, and software applications.

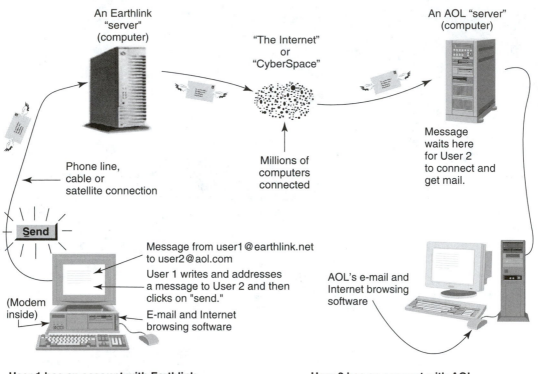

User 1 has an account with Earthlink.
Earthlink is User 1's ISP (Internet Service Provider).

User 2 has an account with AOL.
AOL is User 2's ISP (Internet Service Provider).

Figure 32.1

Life of an e-mail message.

WHAT DO YOU KNOW?

1. Who is User 1's Internet service provider (ISP)?

2. What is User 1's e-mail address?

3. Who is User 2's ISP?

4. What is User 2's e-mail address?

5. What small piece of equipment is inside User 1's computer that allows her computer to connect to a phone line or cable or satellite?

6. What is a server?

7. What symbol in an e-mail address tells you that it is an e-mail address rather than a Web site address?

8. Which of the following best summarizes the path of User 1's e-mail message to User 2? The message goes out of User 1's e-mail program through a phoneline (or other connection):
    (a) to AOL to Earthlink to User 2's computer
    (b) to Earthlink to AOL to User 2's computer
    (c) direct from User 1's computer to User 2's computer
    (d) to AOL to User 2's computer

HOW DID YOU DO?

1. Earthlink
2. user1@earthlink.net
3. AOL
4. user2@aol.com
5. the modem
6. a computer, faster and larger than most individual users' computers
7. the @ ("at") symbol
8. (b). When User 1 clicks the "Send" button, the message goes through the modem, through the phone line (or cable or other connection) to Earthlink's (her Internet service provider's) server. That server reads the address and sends it through the Internet to AOL. The message waits on an AOL server until User 2 connects to AOL to get the mail waiting there for him.

TERMS RELATED TO E-MAIL

ISP   Internet service provider; a company that provides users with a connection that allows them to send and receive e-mail and browse the Internet; examples of a few of the thousands of ISPs are AOL (America Online), MSN, Earthlink, and esva.net

server   also called "host"; a computer through which other computers connect to the Internet

modem   a piece of hardware in a computer or attached to it to which a phone line, cable, or wireless transmitter/receiver is connected and through which a connection to the Internet is established and maintained

T1, DSL, cable, wireless   types of connections to the Internet; T1 and DSL refer to fast types of telephone lines; cable refers to high-speed cable, similar to television cable; wireless refers to a satellite connection

e-mail   electronic mail

> **e-mail client or program**   the e-mail software program used by individual e-mail users; the most popular mail programs are Eudora, Microsoft Outlook, Netscape Communicator, and the e-mail client used by America Online
>
> **@**   "at"; the symbol in an e-mail address that indicates that it is, indeed, an e-mail address; it is located between the user's identification and the name of the Internet service provider

THE WEB

MEMORANDUM

TO: Marketing Department Staff

SUBJECT: New Web Site Domain Names

We have just registered three new domain names, which we shall use for the new Web sites we are building for the new juice product, Joosey Juice. The domain names we have registered are jooseyjuice.com, jooseyjuice.biz, and jooseyjuice.net. We are also considering registration of the domain name jooseyjuice.org for our nonprofit sister company. Other extensions such as .mil (military), .gov (government), and .edu (educational institution) are, of course, not appropriate for us.

The Web sites will have approximately 20 Web pages each. The sites will have a substantial number of links to other sites for nutrition education, fun and games for young children, and plant science, particularly regarding fruit trees. Furthermore, each site will include a page for staff news and updates. The URL for the

staff page on jooseyjuice.com will be

http://www.jooseyjuice.com/staffupdates.htm.

WHAT DO YOU KNOW?

Circle the letter next to the best answer for each question. Use the context clues in the preceding memo to help you decide.

1. Which of the following is an example of a domain name?
   (a) http://www.shoesforfitness.com
   (b) shoesforfitness
   (c) shoesforfitness.com
   (d) .com

2. Which of the following is true about Web page links?
   (a) Web pages can have many links to many other Web pages.
   (b) There are probably billions of links on the Web.
   (c) Links can give users easy access to a great deal of additional information.
   (d) All of the above

3. Which of the following choices is an example of a domain name extension?
   (a) /pageone.htm
   (b) pageone.com
   (c) .com
   (d) domainname.com

4. Which of the following is an example of a URL?
   (a) http://www.saladdays.net/romainelettuce.htm
   (b) saladdays.net
   (c) saladdays
   (d) romainelettuce.htm

5. Which of the following statements is true?
   (a) Domain names are registered so that any given domain name cannot be assigned to two different people or companies.
   (b) A Web site may have many Web pages.
   (c) The graphics on a Web page have their own URL.
   (d) All of the above

HOW DID YOU DO?

1. (c). Only shoesforfitness.com is a domain name. The first choice contains the domain name, but it is a complete Web page address, a URL. The second choice is not a domain name because it is missing the extension. The fourth choice is not a domain name; it is only an extension.

2. (d). All of these statements are true about links.

3. (c). The extension of a domain name consists of the two or three characters following the dot in the domain name.

4. (a). A URL is the complete, specific, and unique address of a Web page or image or other element of a Web site.

5. (d). All of these statements are true. Read the following definitions for further clarification.

TERMS RELATED TO THE WEB

Web site   an organized, related, interconnected group of Web pages. Sites typically include a "home page," which is the first page seen by someone entering the site, and subsequent pages which are usually reachable from the home page and other internal links.

Web page   a page on a Web site. Every Web page is identified by a unique address, or URL. A printed page is usually 11 inches long, but Web pages can be very long indeed, and can take up many paper pages when printed.

domain name   the main part of an Internet address, including its extension. In the address http://www.disney.com/news/pocahontas.htm, for example, "disney.com" is the domain name. Until late 1999, domain names were limited to 26 characters; now they may include as many as 67 characters.

extension   the two- or three-letter suffix portion of a domain name, the most familiar of which is .com, pronounced "dot com."
   Domain name extensions indicate the "top-level domain" (TLD) to which the name belongs. For example: .com indicates a commercial business; .net indicates a company that specializes in networks; .gov is used by government sites, local, state, or national; .org indicates an organization, usually nonprofit; .edu is used by educational institutions and institutes, school districts, and schools; .mil is used by the military. Some extensions indicate the country where the site is based—.mx for Mexico or .ca for Canada, for example. In 2000 and 2001, .md was added for use by physicians, hospitals, and other medical-related entities, .biz as an alternative for business sites, .ent for entertainment sites, and .per for personal sites.

domain name registration   reservation of a main Internet site address (domain name) with Internic, more recently called Network Solutions, or other entity officially authorized to regulate assignment of domain names.

URL   acronym for "Universal Resource Locator"; the exact World Wide Web address of Web pages, Web images, documents, and other Web resources.

Each page and graphic on the Internet has its own URL. The URL of the Burpee's logo on its home page is: http://www.burpee.com/image/global/wwwlogo.gif.

Learn more about URLs at http://www.w3.org/Addressing/Addressing.html.

link   a connection between a location on a page and another location, on the same or a different page on the Internet. When a user clicks a link, the location connected to the link is displayed. Text links are often underlined and often blue. Graphics can also be linked. When the mouse is pointed at a link, the mouse pointer usually changes to a pointing hand.

Working with Words

MULTIPLE CHOICE

Circle the letter next to the answer that best completes the sentence.

1. The acronym *ISP* stands for _____.
    (a) Internet Source Protection
    (b) Internet Service Protection
    (c) Internet Service Provider
    (d) International Standards Provisions

2. A modem is _____.
    (a) a gizmo in or attached to a computer that a phone line or cable connects to
    (b) a modern mode of computing
    (c) a host computer
    (d) a network

3. The symbol in an e-mail address that tells you it is an e-mail address rather than a Web site is _____.
    (a) $
    (b) a dot
    (c) @
    (d) http://

4. When a user clicks the "Send" button to send an e-mail message, the message _____.
    (a) goes to the sender's ISP server first
    (b) goes to the recipient's ISP server first
    (c) goes directly into the recipient's computer
    (d) none of the above

5. Which of the following is an example of a domain name?
    (a) .net
    (b) harrylumpkin.net
    (c) harrylumpkin
    (d) http://www.harrylumpkin.net

6. Which of the following is an example of a domain name extension?
    (a) .net
    (b) harrylumpkin.net
    (c) harrylumpkin
    (d) http://www.harrylumpkin.net

7. Which of the following is an example of a Universal Resource Locator?
    (a) .net
    (b) harrylumpkin.net
    (c) harrylumpkin
    (d) http://www.harrylumpkin.net

8. A link on a Web page _____.
    (a) takes users to the page or part of a page being linked to
    (b) lets that page read all the information on the user's computer
    (c) is always indicated by an image of a little chain
    (d) none of the above

FIND THE MISFIT

In each group, underline the word or phrase that does not belong with the others. Then state why it doesn't belong.

1. modem, software, equipment, connection

2. extension, domain name, link, URL

3. AOL, ISP, URL, server

4. e-mail, @, send, URL

5. server, computer, user, host

6. dot com, http://, .edu, extension

7. Web address, e-mail address, URL, Universal Resource Locator

8. Web, spider, Internet, World Wide Web

USING YOUR WORDS

Use each of the following words or phrases in a sentence that demonstrates that you understand the meaning of the word or phrase.

1. ISP

2. server

3. modem

4. T1 line

5. URL

6. extension

7. ISP

8. domain name

9. http://www.cnn.com

10. link

The Internet 2

SEARCH ENGINES

Search engines are an important tool for finding information on the Web.

MEMORANDUM

TO: Jim Prain, Web Site Assistant

FROM: Joan Kelly

Our new Web site for Joosey Juice is fabulous!
Unfortunately, I worry that no one will ever see it.
This morning I checked the major Internet portal sites
serving our industry, and our site was not listed in any
of them. Then I searched for our products with logical
keywords, including "juice" and "fruit juice," using
Yahoo!, Google, Excite, and a few other search engines,
and again our site was not among the results.

```
Please register the URL of the main page of our Web

site with all major portals and search engines

immediately so that they will spider our pages as soon

as possible. How long will it take the robots and

spiders to spider our pages so that we show up in search

results?
```

WHAT DO YOU KNOW?

Circle the letter next to the answer that best completes the sentence. Use the context clues in the preceding memo to help you decide.

1. Spiders _____.
   (a) travel the Internet to ruin Web pages
   (b) read Web pages and take information back to search engines
   (c) create links that hold the Web together
   (d) none of the above

2. Keywords _____.
   (a) are entered into search engines or portals by users looking for information on the Internet
   (b) are the text on Web sites about locksmiths
   (c) are part of a domain name
   (d) none of the above

3. On the Internet, a portal is _____.
   (a) a Web site about doors and gates
   (b) a hotel site
   (c) a site or page that users visit to look for information
   (d) none of the above

4. Web site owners complete URL registrations so that _____.
   (a) search engines will include them in their information given to users
   (b) the site is a legal entity
   (c) the URL cannot be spidered
   (d) none of the above

> ### HOW DID YOU DO?
>
> 1. (b). Spiders are automated programs that retrieve information from Web sites and send it back to the search engine or portal that sent them out.
> 2. (b). Most portals and search engines have an area for visitors to enter keywords and then click a button to ask for a list of Web sites related to those words.
> 3. (c). A portal is a "gateway to the Internet."
> 4. (a). Some search engines will find some sites without the site's URL or URLs being registered. However, URL registration helps assure that the site will be found and spidered and the information entered in the search engine's database.

TERMS RELATED TO SEARCH ENGINES

keywords   words people enter into search engines to find information on the Web. Most search engines match words being searched for with Web pages that have them.

portal   an Internet site offering a selection of resources and services, such as e-mail, links to popular Web sites, search engines, directories, shopping malls, promotions, chat rooms, free Web pages, etc. Many major search engines, such as Yahoo!, Excite, and Infoseek, are now portals.

search engine   an Internet site, function, or program that maintains databases of Internet pages, their keywords, and their URLs, and retrieves the information according to keywords entered by users, displaying a list of Internet sites and/or pages. Examples include Excite, Infoseek, Google, and Webcrawler.

spider, robot   a program that automatically retrieves Web page information for use by search engines. Some Web pages have hidden text telling spiders what to do, for example, "return every 7 days," or "do not catalog this page." To *spider* means to crawl through a Web site getting information. (Robots or spiders do spidering—not people.)

URL registration   submission of a Web site's URL and sometimes a short description of the site to a search engine, directory, or portal so that the site will be listed in the directory and/or reported by the search engine.

WEB SITE EXTRAS

Web sites are increasingly sophisticated and complicated and can have many features and functions.

MEMORANDUM

TO: Jim Prain, Web Site Assistant

FROM: Joan Kelly

Please make the following additions to our Joosey Juice Web site.

1. A CGI form specifically for buyers of Joosey Juice to report their product satisfaction to us. Make the form an easy-to-use survey with no more than four questions.

2. A guest book so that our Web site visitors can enter their comments about the site.

3. A Web cam transmission from the factory so that Web visitors can see live shots of Joosey Juice being made and bottled.

4. An e-mail link on every page so that users can click and have our e-mail address entered automatically in an e-mail message from them to us.

WHAT DO YOU KNOW?

Circle T or F to indicate whether each of the following sentences is true or false. Use the context clues in the preceding memo to help you decide.

T F   1. A CGI form is something users can complete on the Internet and then submit to the site owner.

T F   2. A guest book on a Web site is very similar to a guest book at an open house or other event.

T F   3. A Web cam is an automated function that makes a Web site operate properly.

T F   4. E-mail links make communicating with the owners or managers of a Web site more convenient for users.

HOW DID YOU DO?

1. True. A CGI form is a form. CGI forms can be various types of forms—surveys, quizzes, polls, order forms, and so on.

2. True. A guest book is a guest book.

3. False. A Web cam is a camera connected to a Web page.

4. True. Many businesses put e-mail links on each page of their site so that visitors can contact them easily.

TERMS RELATED TO WEB SITE EXTRAS

CGI form   a form on a Web page that Internet users can fill in and that is then sent to the owner of the Web site or some other designated recipient. When you complete a guest book or a survey on the Internet, you are often filling in a CGI form. CGI is an acronym for Common Gateway Interface.

guest book   a particular type of CGI form that users complete to say they've visited a site and leave comments

e-mail link   a link on a Web page that opens a user's message composition window with the recipient's address already entered.

Web cam   a camera that is linked to a Web site in such a way that the site's visitors can see what the camera is viewing. Some Web cams are "live," that is, continuously refreshing; others refresh every few seconds.

Working with Words

MULTIPLE CHOICE

Circle the letter next to the answer that best completes the sentence.

1. So that site visitors can e-mail us easily, please _____.
    - (a) display our e-mail address on the front page of the site
    - (b) place an e-mail link on each page of the site
    - (c) place a CGI form on each page of the site
    - (d) place a link to a CGI form on each page of the site

2. Internet users usually go to a portal site to _____.
    - (a) get the weather forecast
    - (b) find other sites with needed information
    - (c) get ocean travel information
    - (d) order wine

3. An online survey could be a type of _____.
    - (a) guest book
    - (b) search engine
    - (c) portal
    - (d) CGI form

4. A search engine _____.
    - (a) is owned by a railroad
    - (b) drives the Internet
    - (c) helps users find information
    - (d) none of the above

FIND THE MISFIT

In each group, underline the word or phrase that does not belong with the others. Then state why it doesn't belong.

1. robot, spider, spin, search engine

2. search engine, Web cam, keyword, portal

3. survey, guest book, spider, CGI form

4. URL registration, license, search engine, spider

5. crawl, retrieve, spider, CGI

USING YOUR WORDS

Use each of the following words or phrases in a sentence that demonstrates that you understand the meaning of the word or phrase.

1. search engine

2. spider

3. CGI form

4. Web cam

5. e-mail link

6. keywords

7. URL registration

8. Yahoo!

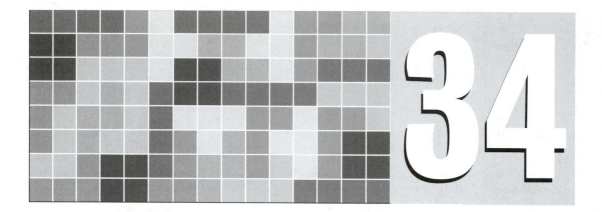

Leadership and Group Input

The terms you will become familiar with in this chapter are related to human relations, or the study of interactions between people, particularly between people in the workplace. We'll begin by examining types of leaders and leadership. Then we'll work with terminology related to types of organizational structures and communications within organizations.

LEADERSHIP

Letter from Executive Search Firm

Dear Ms. Downing,

We have found two highly qualified candidates for you

to consider for the position of executive vice presi-

dent. Your description of the desired person stressed

that leadership ability is the main quality you are

looking for. Both candidates have extensive leadership ability, that is, they can influence others to achieve goals or perform in a certain manner.

However, after interviewing each candidate at length, we have concluded that the two individuals are very different types of leaders. One is a transactional leader who is task-oriented and tends to focus intensely on roles and tasks, and greatly values clarity in task requirements and performance. The other is a transformational leader, more person-oriented, and leads by inspiring and motivating those involved to do their best for the good of the company.

In our opinion, your company has reached a stage in its growth and development where it will benefit most from the transformational leader. Nonetheless, we have enclosed the files on both candidates and will make appointments for you to meet them at your convenience.

WHAT DO YOU KNOW?

Circle T or F to indicate whether each of the following statements is true or false. Use the context clues in the preceding letter to help you decide.

T F   1. Leaders influence others.

T F   2. All leaders behave the same way.

T F   3. A transactional leader tends to focus on personal transactions.

T F   4. A transformational leader is more person-oriented than a transactional leader.

T F   5. People are more likely to be inspired by a transactional leader.

HOW DID YOU DO?

1. True. One key characteristic of a leader is that he or she can influence others to behave in certain ways and motivate them to achieve goals.
2. False. Leaders vary considerably in their approaches to leadership. Two types of leaders discussed in the letter are the transactional leader and the transformational leader.
3. False. A transactional leader tends to focus on task requirements.
4. True. Transformational leaders focus on people more than tasks.
5. False. Transactional leaders are not generally inspirational. They tend to lead by clarifying roles and tasks.

TERMS RELATED TO LEADERSHIP

leadership   ability to influence others to act in a certain way; leaders guide or inspire others to accept challenges and achieve goals

transactional leaders   leaders who guide others by clarifying roles and task requirements

transformational leaders   leaders who inspire others to act for the good of the organization

LEADERSHIP STYLES

Report to Leader Search Committee

Dear Committee Members:

We asked the final four candidates for your leadership position to complete a questionnaire about their leadership style. A sample of the items and the responses from the four candidates are shown below. The candidates were asked to mark the items that are "like me." The checkmarks in the boxes indicate which items each candidate marked.

SAMPLE ITEMS CANDIDATES :	1	2	3	4
1. Trust groups to make good decisions on their own			√	√
2. Allow workers total freedom in their work				√
3. Let workers use their own judgment in most things		√	√	√
4. Cope well with delays				√
5. Test ideas with followers		√	√	√
6. Make decisions after hearing group input		√		
7. Make decisions jointly with group members			√	
8. Establish uniform procedures for workers to follow	√			
9. Keep work moving quickly at all times	√			
10. Schedule the tasks to be done	√			
11. Make key decisions without much group input	√			
12. Assume responsibility for even small details	√			

Based on these results, we have made the following conclusions about the leadership styles of the four candidates:

- Candidate 1 uses a highly autocratic leadership style. He or she likes to make decisions without group input, likes to be in control of all aspects of workers tasks, likes uniformity, and is more task-oriented than person-oriented.

- Candidates 2, 3, and 4 all use some level of a participative leadership style.

- Candidate 2 uses a consultative participative leadership style. Notice that he or she makes final decisions after hearing group input.

- Candidate 3 uses a democratic participative leadership style. Notice that he or she gives followers a voice by making decisions with them jointly.

- Candidate 4 uses a *laissez-faire* participative leadership style. He or she allows workers the greatest degree of freedom and decision-making power.

WHAT DO YOU KNOW?

Circle T or F to indicate whether each of the following statements is true or false. Use the context clues in the preceding report to help you decide.

T F   1. Autocratic leaders make key decisions without much input from others.

T F   2. Democratic and consultative leadership styles are two kinds of participative leadership.

T F   3. A leader with the consultative style tends to consult with the group to get information and then make the ultimate decision himself or herself.

T F   4. Leaders with a *laissez-faire* leadership style are probably fairly relaxed and easygoing.

T F   5. A leader with the democratic leadership style tends to let others have a voice or "vote" in decision making.

HOW DID YOU DO?

1. True. *Auto-* means "self." *-Crat-* comes from the Greek word for "power." An autocratic leader holds the power himself or herself. These leaders do not seek much input from followers.

2. True. Participative leadership refers to styles of leadership that involve followers in some way or other—from strictly providing information to actually making decisions.

3. True. Consultative leaders do consult with the group. They do not give the group the power to make the decision, however.

4. True. *Laissez-faire* leaders are the leaders who give the most decision-making power to the group.

5. True. Democratic leaders give some power to the group. The group has a say in the decision. Remember that the prefix *demo-* means "people."

TERMS RELATED TO LEADERSHIP STYLES

participative leadership style   a style of leadership that actively seeks input from followers regarding, for example, developing plans, problem solving, and decision making; three types of participative leadership style are the consultative, democratic, and *laissez-faire* styles

consultative leadership style   a participative leadership style that seeks input from followers but does not give them a "vote"; decisions are made by the leader

democratic leadership style   a participative leadership style that allows followers to have a voice or influence in the decision-making process; decisions are made by the leader and the group

laissez-faire leadership style   also called *free-reign leadership style;* a participative leadership style that allows followers to make their own decisions in matters that affect them; decisions are made by the group, with input from the leader and assistance when needed

autocratic leadership style   the style of a taskmaster who makes all decisions and tells others what to do

---

GROUP INPUT

Some of the types of leadership discussed in the previous sections rely on group input. Many decisions in the workplace are made in groups—committees, taskforces, panels, and teams, for example.

MEMORANDUM

TO: Members of the Scheduling Committee

FROM: Kevin Fischman

SUBJECT: Committee Meetings

We will meet Tuesday at 9:00 A.M. in the large conference room

for a brainstorming session. The goal of the session will be to

generate ideas for resolving the scheduling problems and minimize the need for overtime. All ideas are encouraged. No criticisms of ideas will be permitted at this meeting. The ideas will
be recorded for later discussion and evaluation.

On Wednesday at 9:00 A.M. we will meet again in the large
conference room. The goals for Wednesday's meeting are (a) to
evaluate the ideas from the previous day, and (b) to try to
reach consensus about the best way to solve the scheduling problems. During this consensus-building meeting, we encourage all
evaluative comments. Please do not keep silent if you do not
agree with what is being said. We need your input, and this type
of groupthink is an obstacle to putting everyone's experience
and knowledge to work on the issue.

WHAT DO YOU KNOW?

Circle T or F to indicate whether each of the following statements is true or false. Use the context clues in the preceding memo to help you decide.

T F   1. Brainstorming is a form of mental confusion.
T F   2. *Consensus* refers to counting votes.
T F   3. Groupthink is a form of group decision making.
T F   4. *Consensus building* refers to attempting to formulate a solution or decision that is acceptable to most of the group.

HOW DID YOU DO?

1. False. Brainstorming is a technique for generating as many ideas as possible from a group.
2. False. *Consensus* refers to agreement. Remember from your work on prefixes that *con-* means "together." The root *-sent-* means "thinking." *Consensus* means "thinking together", or, more accurately, "thinking alike."
3. False. *Groupthink* is a term that describes an individual's reluctance to speak out against the ideas of a group. The individual goes along with the group's thinking, even though he or she does not agree. Groupthink is an obstacle to effective idea generation and consensus building.
4. True. *Building consensus* means "building agreement among the members of a group."

TERMS RELATED TO GROUP INPUT

brainstorming   a technique sometimes used to build consensus that involves generation of suggestions and alternatives without criticism; the alternatives are recorded for discussion and analysis, at which time evaluation and criticism of the ideas are permitted

consensus   agreement on an issue or point by everyone in a group

consensus building   attempting to develop a decision or solution that is acceptable to everyone or almost everyone in a group; working to find acceptable compromises

groupthink   a tendency to hold back unpopular views; groupthink gives the appearance of agreement or conformity

Working with Words

MULTIPLE CHOICE

Circle the letter next to the answer that best completes the sentence.

1. Nancy did not agree with the ideas proposed in the committee meeting, but she did not want to appear to disagree with the group, so she did not speak up. This is an example of _____.
   - (a) consensus building
   - (b) groupthink
   - (c) compromising
   - (d) brainstorming

2. A _____ leadership style seeks input from followers but does not give them a vote.
   - (a) participative
   - (b) democratic
   - (c) consultative
   - (d) consultative participative

3. The ability to influence others to act in a certain way is one description of _____.
   - (a) bossiness
   - (b) groupthink
   - (c) leadership
   - (d) *laissez-faire*

4. Mike Anthony made most decisions without input from his work teams. Mike would be called _____.
   - (a) an autocratic leader
   - (b) a consultative leader
   - (c) a bureaucrat
   - (d) a democrat

5. The most easygoing, hands-off leadership style is the _____ style.
   - (a) *laissez-faire*
   - (b) analytical
   - (c) consultative
   - (d) democratic

6. Transactional leaders are likely to focus on _____.
   - (a) tasks
   - (b) time
   - (c) people
   - (d) rewards

FIND THE MISFIT

In each group, underline the word that does not belong with the others. Then state why it doesn't belong.

1. consensus, groupthink, agreement, compromise

2. participative, autocratic, consultative, democratic

3. leadership, consensus, transactional, transformational

4. transactional, roles, transformational, tasks

5. motivational, transformational, tasks, inspirational

6. control, taskmaster, *laissez-faire*, autocratic

USING YOUR WORDS

Use each of the following words or phrases in a sentence that demonstrates that you understand the meaning of the word or phrase.

1. consensus

2. leadership

3. consultative participative leadership style

4. groupthink

5. autocratic

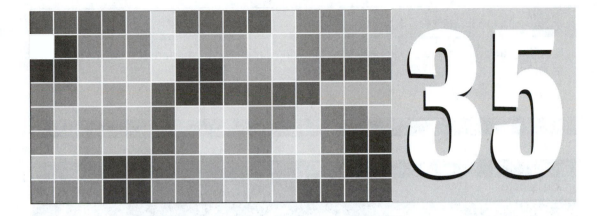

Shipping

Almost all businesses ship or receive goods of some sort—equipment, supplies, parts, and finished products or merchandise. A very few companies have their own trucks or railroads or airplanes or ships to carry their goods to destination. Most businesses use some type of transportation company to ship their goods. The most commonly known to consumers are the U.S. Postal Service, United Parcel Service, FedEx, Roadway, Consolidated Freightways, and the railroads. In this lesson you will learn terms associated with the shipping of goods.

CONSIGNING

You work in the shipping department of Nesbit's Nuts and Bolts. Your boss tells you to send a 120-pound crate of large bolts to Allied Nails and Screws. The boss says to consign the crate to Emerald Cargo Company, who will transport the shipment to Allied.

WHAT DO YOU KNOW?

Based on this information, complete the following simplified form, part of a *waybill* or *bill of lading*.

Bill of Lading

FROM	
Consignor	
TO	
Consignee	
Ship by	
Carrier	
Contents	
Commodity	
Weight	

HOW DID YOU DO?

1. Consignor: Nesbit's Nuts and Bolts. The consignor is the shipper of the goods.
2. Consignee: Allied Nails and Screws. The consignee is the intended recipient of the shipment.
3. Carrier: Emerald Cargo Company. The carrier is the company that transports the shipment.
4. Commodity: bolts. The commodity is the type of goods being shipped.
5. Weight: 120 pounds.

TERMS RELATED TO CONSIGNING

cargo   goods transported or to be transported, other than mail; also called *freight*

consign   to give or entrust a shipment

consignee   the person or company to whom a shipment is addressed; the recipient of a shipment

consignor   the shipper; the person or company that is sending a shipment

consignment, shipment   a package or group of packages being sent to one recipient from one shipper at one time

commodity   the type of goods being shipped

> **waybill/bill of lading**   the document that accompanies a shipment showing the information about that shipment, including shipper, consignee, billing party, commodity, weight, type of service, insurance, legal information, and so on
>
> **carrier**   the company that transports the shipment; the carrier could be a trucker, railroad, airline, or ocean shipping line

CONSOLIDATING

Read the following description. Try to picture what is happening to the shipments step-by-step. Pay attention to the words in italics.

Carla's Cargo Company had its cartage trucks pick up shipments from twenty-one different companies in Chicago that were going to various cities. Carla's driver took all the cargo to the dock and grouped them according to their destination cities. Four large boxes and nine smaller ones were going to consignees in Los Angeles. The dockworkers loaded the 13 pieces into a *container*, making a single consolidated shipment, or *consolidation*, going to Los Angeles. They made a list, or *manifest*, of all the pieces that went into the container, including the waybill numbers of the shipments, the weight of each piece, and other information. Then they took the container to the airport and sent it to Los Angeles via an airline. In Los Angeles their drivers picked it up, took it to their dock, checked to make sure that all the pieces listed on the manifest had arrived in good shape, and then sorted out the boxes for the *cartage* drivers to deliver to the various consignees.

WHAT DO YOU KNOW?

From the following list, select the word that best completes each sentence and write the word in the blank space provided.

cartage   container   consolidation   manifest

1. The combining of shipments for transportation to a given destination is called a _____.

2. The local pickup, hauling, and delivery of goods from one place to another is called _____.

3. A list of waybills for shipments that are traveling together is called a _____.

4. The shipments that were all headed for Los Angeles were loaded together into a _____.

HOW DID YOU DO?

1. consolidation. Remember from the lessons on prefixes that the prefix *con-* means "together." The root *-solid-* means exactly that, "solid." A consolidation is a combination, or things put together.

2. cartage. The root of this word is *cart-,* which means "to haul." Cartage refers to hauling.

3. manifest. In transportation, a manifest is a list of shipments or passengers. In general usage the term means to show or display, so we have a showing or itemization of the cargo or passengers.

4. container. The various pieces of freight headed for one destination are loaded into a single container.

TERMS RELATED TO CONSOLIDATING

cartage   local transportation of shipments from a shipper's location to the carrier or from a carrier to the consignee's location; also called *haulage*

manifest   a list of all the shipments in a consolidation, container, trailer, railroad car, aircraft, or ship

consolidation   a group of shipments going from one origin to one destination that are weighed together for purposes of cost control

container   a sturdy piece of equipment designed for holding goods being shipped

Working with Words

MULTIPLE CHOICE

Circle the letter next to the answer that best completes the sentence.

1. Charlotte prepared a _____ for the crate she was shipping to her customer.
   - (a) manifest
   - (b) container
   - (c) waybill
   - (d) consolidation

2. When George checked the pieces against the _____, he discovered that a box was missing.
   - (a) manifest
   - (b) carrier
   - (c) container
   - (d) consignee

3. The large crate was being shipped to ABC Lumber. ABC Lumber was the _____.
   - (a) shipper
   - (b) consignee
   - (c) consignor
   - (d) consolidator

4. Fred's Fine Lighting sent six lamps to Ingrid's Interiors. Fred's was the _____.
   - (a) commodity
   - (b) consignor
   - (c) carrier
   - (d) consolidator

5. What type of _____ is in that crate?
   - (a) carrier
   - (b) waybill
   - (c) manifest
   - (d) commodity

6. How many shipments are in the _____?
   - (a) commodity
   - (b) consolidation
   - (c) consignee
   - (d) waybill

7. How many _____ are listed on the _____?
   - (a) waybills   manifest
   - (b) manifests   waybill
   - (c) consignees   commodity
   - (d) carriers   cartage

8. The _____ driver took the freight from the dock to the customer's warehouse.
   - (a) commodious
   - (b) cartage
   - (c) consignment
   - (d) commodity

FIND THE MISFIT

In each group, underline the word that does not belong with the others. Then state why it doesn't belong.

1. list, manifest, manifold, itemization

2. combination, hardening, consolidation, group

3. carriage, haulage, wheel barrow, cartage

4. signature, consignor, shipper, sender

5. consignee, co-signer, recipient, receiver

6. airline, railroad, carrier, consignment

7. accommodation, commodity, goods, material

8. waybill, transportation document, check, shipping form

USING YOUR WORDS

Use each of the following words in a sentence that demonstrates that you understand the meaning of the word.

1. consolidation

2. container

3. cartage

4. consignee

5. waybill

6. carrier

7. manifest

8. commodity

9. cargo

10. consignor

Section 5 Review

The lessons in Section 5 presented words and phrases from the business world. Familiarity with these and other terms that are commonly encountered in work environments will be especially useful to those who are preparing to enter the job market.

The areas addressed by these lessons—human resources, sales, marketing, accounting, finance, computing, the Internet, leadership, and shipping—are areas that you are likely to encounter, regardless of the type of company you work for. Most businesses have departments in each of these areas, although very small companies may have an individual rather than an entire department do the work.

Working with Words

FIND THE MISFIT

In each group, underline the word that does not belong with the others. Then state why it doesn't belong.

1. discharge, terminate, compensate, end

2. payable, cell, bill, invoice

3. marketing, accounting, invoice, personnel

4. competence, incentive, versatility, initiative

5. spider, database, search engine, portal

6. assets, loan, interest, promissory note

7. bargain, negotiate, compensation, discuss

8. remuneration, compensation, reimbursement, termination

9. spreadsheet, rows, invoices, cells

10. location, brand, differentiation, positioning

FILL IN THE BLANKS

From the following list, select the word that best completes each sentence and write the word in the blank space provided. Use each word only once. Use all of the words.

barter	differentiation
compensation	discriminate
human resources	severance
market segment	terminate
promissory note	URL
seniority	waybill

1. The firm was forced to _____ ten of its employees when it closed the branch outside the city.

2. The staff members who lost their jobs when the branch office closed were given _____ pay by the firm.

3. Employees who have worked for a company the longest have _____.

4. Please complete the _____ with the information on that shipment.

5. They decided to _____—Gary built the Web site for his dentist in return for the new crown.

6. The _____ department will be able to answer your questions about the company's vacation policy.

7. If you'll send me the _____ for that Web site, I'll check it out.

8. George signed a _____ when he borrowed the money for his new acoustical guitar.

9. An Equal Opportunity Employer does not _____ in hiring for reasons of race, creed, color, or gender.

10. What is the amount of _____ that her new job pays?

11. Which _____ are you trying to reach with that advertising?

12. The product's _____ is its low price.

WORD SELECTION

Circle the word or phrase in parentheses that best completes the sentence.

1. The firm gave Jose an increase in (compensation / competence).
2. Beverly is able to do many types of tasks; that is, she is a (versatile / verbal) individual.
3. Larry received (compensation / severance) pay when the company terminated him.
4. The bike shop buys its bikes (wholesale / retail) and sells them (wholesale; retail).

5. The firm owed the print shop $2,700 but decided to (defer / reimburse) payment for sixty days.
6. The company (segmented / differentiated) its products as being faster and cleaner.
7. Please (remit / revoke) payment within ten days.
8. Please (reimburse / reinstate) me for the expenses of my last business trip as soon as possible.
9. Use a (spider / search engine) to find information on those vitamins.
10. The database file on that product contains 430 (modems / records).
11. The team will meet at 10:00 Friday for a (brainstorming / consensus) session about the next sales promotion.
12. The local (cartage / commodity) company will deliver the equipment.

WORD GROUP ASSIGNMENTS

Make three groups of words from the following list. Each group should consist of three words that are most like each other. Use each word only once. Use all of the words.

compensation	competent	incentive
motivation	pay	skilled
proficient	remuneration	offer

1. _____

2. _____

3. _____

USING YOUR WORDS (REVIEW)

For each of the following words or phrases, write *either* a sentence using the word or phrase correctly *or* a brief explanation of its use.

1. compensation

2. negotiate

3. Equal Opportunity Employer

4. versatile

5. proficient

6. terminate

7. seniority

8. sales promotion

9. incentive

10. wholesale

11. retail

12. barter

13. consultative selling

14. market segment

15. brand

16. differentiation

17. competitor

18. payable

19. invoice

20. remit

21. allocate

22. reimburse

23. assets

24. liabilities

25. balance sheet

26. principal

27. promissory note

28. return on investment

29. portfolio

30. word processing

31. font

32. merge

33. spreadsheet

34. cell

35. database

36. modem

37. e-mail

38. domain name

39. search engine

40. spider

41. CGI form

42. leadership

43. autocratic leader

44. brainstorm

45. consignee

46. waybill

47. commodity

Working with Words Answer Key

![black bar]

Chapter 1

True or False (1) F, T; (2) F, T; (3) F, T, F; (4) T, T; (5) T, F; (6) F, T; (7) T, F; (8) F, T; (9) F, T; (10) T, T

Fill in the Blanks (1) diverse; (2) constructive; (3) prohibit; (4) obsolete; (5) verify; (6) enhance

Chapter 2

Multiple Choice (1) b; (2) d; (3) a; (4) d; (5) c; (6) c; (7) c; (8) a

Chapter 3

Multiple Choice (1) b; (2) a; (3) c; (4) b; (5) d; (6) a; (7) a; (8) c

Find the Misfit (1) contraction; (2) manage; (3) clues; (4) presence; (5) free

Chapter 4

Multiple Choice (1) c; (2) b; (3) c; (4) a; (5) a; (6) b; (7) a; (8) c; (9) b; (10) a

Fill in the Blanks (1) optional; (2) meticulous; (3) dear; (4) anxiety; (5) prudent; (6) capitulate; (7) proximity; (8) equivalent; (9) competent; (10) irrelevant

Chapter 5

Multiple Choice   (1) b; (2) b; (3) a; (4) c; (5) a; (6) c; (7) b; (8) d; (9) a; (10) c

Find the Misfit   (1) fight; (2) rebut; (3) related; (4) expensive; (5) deteriorate

Chapter 7

Multiple Choice   (1) a; (2) b; (3) d; (4) a; (5) c; (6) c; (7) a; (8) b

Find the Misfit   (1) infer; (2) admit; (3) instruct; (4) state; (5) inform; (7) praise; (8) comprehend; (9) request; (10) comprehend

Fill in the Blanks   (1) apprise; (2) imply; (3) commend; (4) digress; (5) delineate; (6) admonish

Chapter 8

Fill in the Blanks   (1) massive; (2) miniature; (3) diminutive; (4) petty; (5) spacious; (6) minute; (7) enormous; (8) puny

Fill in the Blanks   (1) paltry; (2) petty; (3) abundant; (4) extravagant; (5) adequate; (6) exorbitant; (7) meager; (8) paucity

Find the Misfit   (1) exasperate; (2) pursuit; (3) spacious; (4) minute; (5) old; (6) dim-witted

Chapter 9

Word Selection   (1) essential; (2) paramount; (3) eminent; (4) salient; (5) momentous

Chapter 11

Fill in the Blanks   (1) minimum; (2) unambiguous; (3) ineligible; (4) minimize; (5) dishonest; (6) microscope; (7) nonproductive; (8) maximize

Word Completion   (1) disbelief; (2) unsophisticated; (3) insufficient; (4) megaphone; (5) microscope; (6) macro command

Multiple Choice   (1) a; (2) b; (3) b; (4) b; (5) d; (6) d; (7) a; (8) a

Chapter 12

Word Replacement   (1) multimillion; (2) hypercritical; (3) overpriced; (4) ultramodern; (5) extraordinary; (6) decade; (7) biweekly; (8) multiple

Find the Match   (1) remarkable; (2) ecstatic; (3) everywhere; (4) increase; (5) theory; (6) deprived

Word Selection   (1) semicircle; (2) overqualified; (3) century; (4) extraneous; (5) triplicate; (6) undermine; (7) omnivorous; (8) million

True or False   (1) F; (2) T; (3) T; (4) T; (5) F; (6) T; (7) T; (8) F; (9) T; (10) F

Chapter 13

Fill in the Blanks   (1) pro; (2) intro; (3) ex; (4) circum; (5) per; (6) trans; (7) trans; (8) intro; (9) fore; (10) pre

Multiple Choice   (1) d; (2) c; (3) b; (4) b; (5) c; (6) b

Chapter 14

True or False   (1) F; (2) T; (3) F; (4) T; (5) T; (6) F; (7) F; (8) T; (9) T; (10) F

Find the Misfit   (1) facial; (2) ligature; (3) rude; (4) road; (5) beneficial; (6) sinful

Multiple Choice   (1) b; (2) a; (3) c; (4) b; (5) c; (6) c; (7) a; (8) b

Chapter 15

Fill in the Blanks   (1) requests; (2) visit; (3) inquiries; (4) prescriptions; (5) legible; (6) scribbling; (7) dictates; (8) microscope

Multiple Choice   (1) microscopic; (2) telescopic; (3) circumspect; (4) prescription; (5) subscription; (6) inscription; (7) legible; (8) spectators

Chapter 16

Multiple Choice   (1) a; (2) c; (3) d; (4) a; (5) a; (6) c; (7) b; (8) a

Chapter 17

Multiple Choice   (1) b; (2) b; (3) c; (4) d; (5) a; (6) a; (7) a; (8) c

Fill in the Blanks   (1) ascertain; (2) finish; (3) certain; (4) commemorate; (5) remember; (6) confine; (7) various; (8) finally

Find the Misfit   (1) invariable; (2) varsity; (3) member; (4) locked; (5) curtain; (6) find; (7) confetti; (8) comment

Chapter 18

Multiple Choice   (1) b; (2) b; (3) c; (4) b; (5) a; (6) c; (7) a; (8) b

Fill in the Blanks   (1) illegible; (2) irreversible; (3) invariable; (4) hasty/hastily; (5) carefully; careful; (6) talkative; (7) priceless; (8) joyous; (9) saplings; (10) simplify

Chapter 19

Fill in the Blanks   (1) efficient; (2) contribution; (3) assistant; (4) shipper; (5) cashier; (6) donor; (7) accomplishment; (8) correspondence; (9) Bostonian; (10) grantee

Word Completion   (1) ian/c; (2) eer/h; (3) or/b OR ee/a; (4) ent/g; (5) ee/a OR or/b (whichever was not used for question 3); (6) ant/e; (7) ment/f; (8) er/d

Chapter 21

Multiple Choice   (1) b; (2) d; (3) b; (4) a; (5) c; (6) a; (7) d; (8) b

Find the Misfit   (1) appraisal; (2) affect; (3) excess; (4) alluring; (5) except; (6) computer; (7) except; (8) effect

Fill in the Blanks   (1) access; (2) illusion; (3) accept; (4) effect; (5) allusion; (6) except; (7) excess; (8) affect

Chapter 22

Multiple Choice   (1) council; (2) capitol; (3) antidote; (4) disburse; (5) anecdote; (6) capital; (7) counsel; (8) dispersed

Find the Misfit (1) counsel; (2) disburse; (3) capital; (4) anecdote; (5) counsel; (6) council; (7) capitol; (8) dispersed

Fill in the Blanks (1) antidote; (2) disburse; (3) capitol; (4) anecdote; (5) counsel; (6) council; (7) capital; (8) disperse

Chapter 23

Multiple Choice (1) discrete; (2) uninterested; (3) elicit; (4) eminent; (5) imminent; (6) discreet; (7) disinterested; (8) illicit

Find the Match (1) draw out; (2) prominent; (3) diplomatic; (4) fair; (5) unlawful; (6) about to happen; (7) separate; (8) bored

Fill in the Blanks (1) uninterested; (2) eminent; (3) elicit; (4) discrete; (5) disinterested; (6) illicit; (7) discreet; (8) imminent

Chapter 24

Multiple Choice (1) c; (2) b; (3) a; (4) d; (5) a; (6) c; (7) c; (8) b

Find the Match (1) benefit; (2) required; (3) be ahead; (4) continue; (5) main; (6) rule; (7) permanent; (8) paper

Fill in the Blanks (1) stationary; (2) proceed; (3) precede; (4) perquisite; (5) stationery; (6) principle; (7) principal; (8) prerequisite

Chapter 26

Multiple Choice (1) c; (2) d; (3) c; (4) a; (5) c; (6) d; (7) c; (8) c

Find the Misfit (1) retention; (2) initiative; (3) personnel; (4) salary; (5) race; (6) salary; (7) neat; (8) discriminate

Chapter 27

Fill in the Blanks (1) retail; (2) features and benefits; (3) consultative selling; (4) sales collaterals; (5) wholesale; (6) prospecting; (7) territories; (8) incentive; (9) closing; (10) prospect

Find the Misfit (1) product; (2) physician; (3) customer; (4) manufacturer; (5) telemarketing; (6) cents; (7) sales promotion; (8) follow; (9) closing; (10) territory

Short Answer   (1) fitness progress chart; (2) manufacturer's wholesale prices; (3) 50% off retail; probably (4) yoga tape, dance tapes, nutrition tape, aerobics steps diagram; (5) easy to understand, easy to follow, eat whatever you like

Chapter 28

Fill in the Blanks   (1) segment; (2) research; (3) branding; (4) competitors; (5) demographics; (6) differentiation

Find the Misfit   (1) sell; (2) product features; (3) company name; (4) democracy; (5) partner

Short Answer   (1) Math Crunch and Math Master; (2) parents whose children need help with their math or who want to learn more or practice math; (3) Numbers On! offers value for the dollar; (4) positioned as the fun way to learn math

Chapter 29

Multiple Choice   (1) c; (2) b; (3) a; (4) c; (5) a; (6) c; (7) a; (8) b

Find the Misfit   (1) accrue; (2) reconciliation; (3) asset; (4) receivable

Chapter 30

Word Selection   (1) principal; (2) promissory note; (3) obligor; (4) obligee; (5) interest; (6) collateral; (7) portfolio; (8) investment

Find the Misfit   (1) lender; (2) money; (3) investment; (4) debtor; (5) obligors; (6) interest; (7) portfolio; (8) interest

Chapter 31

Word Selection   (1) spreadsheet; (2) records; (3) cells; (4) font; (5) database; (6) field; (7) word processing; (8) network

Find the Misfit   (1) network; (2) hardware; (3) individuals; (4) database; (5) application; (6) workstation; (7) peripheral; (8) software

Chapter 32

Multiple Choice   (1) c; (2) a; (3) c; (4) a; (5) b; (6) a; (7) d; (8) a

Find the Misfit   (1) equipment; (2) link; (3) URL; (4) URL; (5) user; (6) extension; (7) e-mail address; (8) Spider

Chapter 33

Multiple Choice   (1) b; (2) b; (3) d; (4) c

Find the Misfit   (1) spin; (2) Web cam; (3) spider; (4) license; (5) CGI

Chapter 34

Multiple Choice   (1) b; (2) c; (3) c; (4) a; (5) a; (6) a

Find the Misfit   (1) compromise; (2) autocratic; (3) consensus; (4) transformational; (5) tasks; (6) *laissez-faire*

Chapter 35

Multiple Choice   (1) c; (2) a; (3) b; (4) b; (5) d; (6) b; (7) a; (8) b

Find the Misfit   (1) manifold; (2) hardening; (3) wheel barrow; (4) signature; (5) co-signer; (6) consignment; (7) accommodation; (8) check

Index

T

W